A PART OF ORB

THE GREAT
VALLEY REACHES

Far Snows

Oakenhulls

The Snow Wastes

Seareach Strand

Alone

Goblin's
Teeth Mts

The
Endless
Sea

Ulrik's
Haven

Hilvenmoot

Quench-heart Keep

Alalom

Larandillion

Druath
Glennan

Lightgrieve
Muster

Dvarrowhame

Brigand
keep

Sea
of
the
Star

Castle Eldinarde
Wargrave Abbas

Cow River

Harith-si-
the-Crow

Tower of
Curses

Utter Frith

Burg of Four Friths

Marshes
of Mist

Mts of Vision

Ionalbion

Glastondale
Abbey

Greylap
Hills

Fiendil

Slate Bay

River Baysease

Sundial

The Manmarch

Irsmuncast
nigh Edge

The
Rift

Mortavalon

Aveneg

Doomover

Greyguilds-
on-the-Moor

River Greenbleed

Bay
of
Boreas

Horngroth

Hills

Marshes

Wilderness

The Way of the Tiger
ASSASSIN!

About the authors

Mark Smith was born in Birmingham and brought up in Brighton. He went on to take a degree in experimental psychology at Oxford. Since then he has spent some time in America.

Jamie Thomson was born in Iran and met his co-author whilst at school in Brighton. After taking a degree in politics and government at Kent University he had a variety of jobs before becoming assistant editor of the leading adventure game magazine.

The authors' interest in adventure games began some ten years ago and Mark began work on creating the fantasy world of Orb in 1976.

AVENGER!, the first Way of the Tiger title, is available now. Coming soon – USURPER!

WARNING

Do not attempt any of the techniques or methods
described in this book. They would result in
serious injury or death to an untrained user.

*   *   *

Historical Note

Ninjas are historical fact. Ninjas existed in Japan
from the sixth century AD to the beginning of the
seventeenth century. For much of this period there
were struggles for power between the warlords or
daimios who were the heads of the noble clans.
The Ninjas were unknown faceless men,
professional assassins and spies, killing machines
available for hire. All of the abilities and skills
attributed to the Ninja in this book are based on
reality. Historically, the Ninjas of medieval Japan
were apparently able to perform most of the feats
and were expert in many of the skills outlined in
The Way of the Tiger.

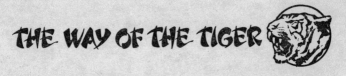

THE WAY OF THE TIGER

ASSASSIN!

Mark Smith and Jamie Thomson

Illustrated by Bob Harvey

KNIGHT BOOKS
Hodder and Stoughton

Copyright © Mark Smith and Jamie Thomson 1985
Illustrations copyright © Hodder and Stoughton Ltd 1985

First published by Knight Books
Second impression 1985

British Library C.I.P.

Smith, Mark
  The way of the tiger II.
  Assassin!
  1. Games – Juvenile literature
  2. Adventure and adventurers – Juvenile literature
  I. Title   II. Thomson, Jamie
  793'.9   GV1203
  ISBN 0 340 377 887

Printed and bound in Great Britain for
Hodder and Stoughton Paperbacks, a
division of Hodder and Stoughton Ltd.,
Mill Road, Dunton Green, Sevenoaks,
Kent (Editorial Office: 47 Bedford
Square, London WC1B 3DP) by
Richard Clay (The Chaucer Press) Ltd.,
Bungay, Suffolk. Photoset by
Rowland Phototypesetting Ltd.,
Bury St Edmunds, Suffolk

NINJA CHARACTER SHEET

COMBAT RATINGS

Punch | 0 | \ | \ | | | | | |

Kick | 0 | v | | | | | | |

Throw | 0 | \ | | | | | | |

Fate Modifier | 0 | | | | | | | |

Inner Force | 5 | | | | | | | |
| | | | | | | | |

Endurance | 20
18
\2
10

SHURIKEN

☆
☆
☆

NINJA TOOLS

Ninja Costume
Breathing Tube
Iron Sleeves
Garotte
Flash Powder
Flint & Tinder
Spiderfish
Blood of Nil

NOTES

Immune to Poisons
Pick lock, Detect & Disarm Traps
Poison Needles

SPECIAL ITEMS

OPPONENT ENCOUNTER BOXES

Name: Keep Guard

Endurance:

Name:

Endurance:

Name:

Endurance:

Name:

Endurance:

Name:

Endurance:

Name:

Endurance:

Name:

Endurance:

Name:

Endurance:

Winged Horse Kick

Leaping Tiger Kick

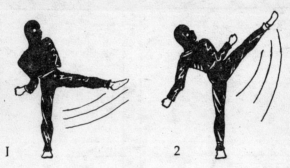

1

2

Forked Lightning Kick

Iron Fist Punch

Tiger's Paw Punch

Cobra Strike
Punch

Whirlpool Throw

Dragon's Tail Throw

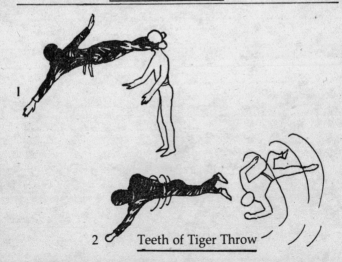

Teeth of Tiger Throw

BACKGROUND

On the magical world of Orb, alone in a sea that the people of the Manmarch call Endless, lies the mystical Island of Tranquil Dreams.

Many years have passed since the time when, as an infant, you first saw its golden shores and emerald rice meadows. A servant brought you, braving the distant leagues of the ponderous ocean, from lands to which you have never returned. Your loyal servant laid you, an orphan, at the steps of the Temple of the Rock praying that the monks would care for you, for she was frail and dying of a hideous curse.

Monks have lived on the island for centuries, dedicated to the worship of their God, Kwon, He who speaks the Holy Words of Power, Supreme Master of Unarmed Combat. They live only to help others resist the evil that infests the world. Seeing that you were alone and needed care, the monks took you in and you became an acolyte at the Temple of the Rock. Nothing was made of the strange birthmark, shaped like a crown which you carry on your thigh, though you remember that the old servant insisted that it was of mystical importance. Whenever you have asked about this the monks have bade you meditate and be patient.

The most ancient and powerful of them all, Naijishi, Grandmaster of the Dawn, became your foster-father. He gave you guidance and training in the calm goodness of Kwon, knowledge of men and their ways and how to meditate so that your mind floats free of your body and rides the winds in search of truth.

From the age of six, however, most of your time has been spent learning the Way of the Tiger. Now, you

11

are a Ninja, a master of the martial arts and a deadly assassin who can kill the most powerful enemies unseen and unsuspected. Like a tiger, you are strong, stealthy, agile, patient in the stalking of prey and deadly. In the Land of Plenty and the Manmarch the fabled Ninja, known as the 'Men with no Shadow', are held in awe – the mere mention of Ninja strikes fear into people's hearts. But you are one of the few who worship Kwon and follow the Way of the Tiger. You use your skill as a bringer of death to rid the world of evil-doers.

At an early age you hung by the hands for hours on end from the branches of trees to strengthen your arms. You ran for miles, your light-footed speed enough to keep a thirty foot ribbon trailing above the ground. You trod tightropes, as agile as a monkey. Now you swim like a fish and leap like a tiger; you move like the whisper of the breeze and glide through the blackest night, like a shade. Before he died Naijishi taught you the Ninja's Covenant.

NINJA NO CHIGIRI

'I will vanish into the night; change my body to wood or stone; sink into the earth and walk through walls and locked doors. I will be killed many times, yet will not die; change my face and become invisible, able to walk among men without being seen.'

It was after your foster-father, Naijishi's death that you began to live the words of the Covenant. A man came to the island, Yaemon, Grandmaster of Flame. Using borrowed sorcery he tricked the monks into believing that he was a worshipper of Kwon from the Great Continent. He was indeed a monk but he worshipped Kwon's twisted brother, Vile, who helps the powerful to subdue the weak, and wicked men to rule fools. Yaemon slew Naijishi – no one could match him in unarmed combat – and he stole the Scrolls of Kettsuin from the Temple. Once more you knew the pain of loss for you had loved Naijishi as a father. You swore an oath to Kwon that one day you would avenge his death. . .

THE MALICE OF THE GODS OF EVIL

As chronicled in the book AVENGER! you used your skills as a hunter and a bringer of death to avenge the killing of Naijishi, your spiritual father. You tracked his murderer, Yaemon, Grandmaster of the evil monks of the Scarlet Mantis to Quench-heart Keep, in the shadow of the Goblin's Teeth Mountains. A Ranger, Glaivas, brought you across the Endless Sea on his ship, the Aquamarin, and you landed at the city of Doomover, in the Manmarch. You travelled hundreds of leagues through the Wilderness, crossing the Mountains of Vision at Fortune Pass, where you were forced to kill Olvar the Chaos-Bringer, a berserk barbarian. Thence you journeyed to the Sea of the Star, to Druath Glennan and now to Quench-heart Keep. Yaemon had stolen the Scrolls of Kettsuin which hold the secret to the Word of Power which would bind your god, Kwon, in Inferno. Two other powerful and evil men had joined him; each knew another such Word of Power, to bind a god or goddess in the lake of boiling blood for eternity.

You stand now, on the rainwashed roof of the Great Keep. You have just killed Yaemon's allies – poisoned Honoric, leader of the dreaded Legion of the Sword of Doom, with the Blood of Nil, and slaughtered Manse the Deathmage, a reverencer of Nemesis, the most powerful of the gods of Evil.

Their bodies lie chill and cold nearby. After a great battle with Yaemon you have now triumphed again and are revenged. With his dying breath he has told you that he was responsible for the death of your true father whom you never knew. Now he lies before you; in death he seems smaller and less imposing than in life. His scarlet jacket, now drenched with rain and sweat, has fallen open to reveal a waxed parchment, the Scrolls of Kettsuin and a map of Orb. You are about to open these when a wondrous feeling of peace overwhelms you and the voice of your god, Kwon, sounds all around you.

'The Grandmaster of the Dawn named you well, Avenger, for now it is Yaemon and not I who will languish in the lake of boiling blood in Inferno. If you had failed, the Doom Legion and the monks of the Scarlet Mantis would have swept across the Manmarch, aided by the priests who revere Nemesis, and all mankind would have lived in terror under the evil overlords you have slain.'

Your wounds are healed as if by a miracle, and new strength floods into your body as the god gives you Inner Force. You feel dazed and awed by what is happening and the sense of Kwon's goodness fills your soul with enlightenment.

'There is little time now, Avenger, for the gods of Evil move against us. You must return the Scrolls of Kettsuin to their rightful place at the Temple of the Rock on the Island of Tranquil Dreams. Your journey will be beset with dangers, but I will aid you. Choose a skill from the Way of the Tiger which you have not yet mastered and I will grant you its knowledge. It shall be as if you had practised it from your birthing.' The god continues, 'I will help you but once, at a time of great danger. If you truly have need of me say only "Kwon, redeem me," and I shall be your salvation. I will watch over you, Avenger, for it is my hope that one day you will join me in the Garden of the gods.'

As Kwon's presence leaves, you cannot stop yourself calling out, 'Who was my real father?' It is as if the wind itself speaks to you as the voice of Kwon fades, 'It is not yet time, Avenger.'

You shrug your shoulders defiantly as the malice of the gods of Evil seems to beat upon your back. They will put many obstacles in your way and you will never see the beautiful Island of Tranquil Dreams again if Fate should turn her back on you. You shiver, noticing the coldness of the rain for the first time. Kwon has departed and you are alone once more.

COMBAT

As a Master of Taijutsu, the Ninja's art of unarmed combat, you have four main ways of fighting: throwing Shuriken (see under 'Skills'), kicks, punches or throws. You will be told when you can use Shuriken.

In general it will be harder to hit an opponent when kicking but a kick will do more damage. A throw, if successful, will allow you to follow up with a possible 'killing blow', but if you fail a throw your Defence against an opponent will be lower, as you are open to attack. Whenever you are in a combat you will be asked which type of attack you wish to make. (See the Way of the Tiger Illustrations for the different types of kicks, punches and throws available to you.) You will be told which paragraph to turn to, depending on your choice. When you are resolving combat, you will find it useful to record your opponent's Defence and Endurance score. A number of Encounter Boxes are provided with your Character Sheet for this purpose.

The combats have been presented in such a way that it is possible for you briefly to examine the rules and begin play almost immediately. However, if you do this, don't forget about Blocking and Inner Force, as you won't be told when to use these in the text.

PUNCH

You will be told what Defence number your opponent has against a punch. Roll two dice, and if the score is higher than his or her Defence number, you have successfully punched your opponent. In this case, roll one more die. The result is the amount of damage you have inflicted on your opponent. Subtract it from his Endurance totals. If this has reduced your opponent's score to 0 or less, you have won. When your opponent attacks you, you will be given your Defence number for that combat. Roll two dice; if the score is greater than this number, you have been hit. The amount of damage inflicted upon you depends on the opponent and will be noted in the paragraph: usually in the format of 'Damage: 1 Die + 1' or '2 Dice' or '1 Die + 2'. Simply roll the required number of dice and add the number given. This is the total damage inflicted upon you. However, before you subtract this score from your Endurance, you may choose to try and block or parry the attack (see Block).

Punch Modifier

Whenever you make a 'Punch Roll' to determine whether or not you have successfully struck an opponent, add or subtract your Punch Modifier. This Modifier reflects your skill in using the punches of the Way of the Tiger. You begin with a Punch Modifier of 0, as noted on your Character Sheet. This will rise as you progress in the Way of the Tiger and may change throughout the adventure.

KICK

The kick and the Kick Modifier work exactly as the punch, except that when you roll the dice to determine the damage you inflict, add 2 to the dice – a kick is more damaging than a punch.

THROW

The throw and Throw Modifier work as the punch. However, if you are successful, no damage is done to your attacker, but you will be allowed another attack, a punch or kick, and it will be much easier to strike a thrown opponent. If you are successful with this, your follow-up attack, add 2 to the damage you inflict.

THE NINJA'S ENDURANCE

You begin the game with 20 points of Endurance. Keep a running total of your Endurance score on your Character Sheet. It will probably be the category that will change most as you are wounded, healed etc. When you reach 0 Endurance or less, you are dead and your adventure ends.

THE BLOCK

As a Ninja, a master of Taijutsu, you have the ability to block or parry incoming blows with various parts of your body, often your forearms. For this purpose, thin, lightweight iron rods have been sewn into your sleeves enabling you to block even swords and other weapons. During combat, if you have been hit, you may try to block the blow and take no damage. Roll two dice. If the score is less than your Defence given in that combat, you have successfully blocked the blow, and you take no damage. If your score is equal to or greater than your Defence, you take damage in the normal way. In any case, because you have taken the time to block, your next attack is less effectual, as your opponent has had more time to react. Whether your block is successful or not, subtract 2 from your Punch, Kick and Throw Modifier for your next attack only. Remember you can only block blows.

INNER FORCE

Through meditation and rigorous training you have mastered the ability to unleash spiritual or inner power through your body in the same way as the karate experts of today break blocks of wood and bricks. In any combat, before you roll the dice to determine if you will hit or miss an opponent, you may choose to use Inner Force. If you do, deduct one point from your Inner Force score. This is used up whether or not you succeed in striking your opponent. If you are successful, however, double the score you roll when determining the amount of damage you inflict. When your Inner Force is reduced to 0, you may no longer use Inner Force. So use it wisely! You begin the game with 5 points of Inner Force.

FATE

Luck plays its part and the goddess Fate has great

power on the world of Orb. Whenever you are asked to make a Fate Roll, roll two dice and add or subtract your Fate Modifier. If the score is 7–12, you are lucky and Fate has smiled on you. If the score is 2–6, you are unlucky and Fate has turned her back on you. You begin your adventure with a Fate Modifier of 0.

THE SKILLS OF THE WAY OF THE TIGER

You have been trained in ninjitsu all of your life. Your senses of smell, sight and hearing have been honed to almost superhuman effectiveness. You are well versed in woodcraft, able to track like a bloodhound, and to cover your own tracks. Your knowledge of plants and herb lore enables you to live off the land. You are at the peak of physical fitness, able to run up to fifty miles a day and swim like a fish. Your training included horsemanship, a little ventriloquism, meditation, the ability to hold yourself absolutely still for hours on end, perfecting your balance, and 'The Seven Ways of Going' or disguise. The latter skill involves comprehensive training so that you can perform as a minstrel, for instance, if this disguise is used. However, a major part of this training has been in stealth, hiding in shadows, moving silently, and breathing as quietly as possible, enabling you to move about unseen and unheard. You begin the game with these skills.

There are nine other skills. One of these, Shuriken-jitsu, is always taught to a Ninja in training. This you must take, but you may then choose three other skills from the remaining eight, and note them down on your Character Sheet.

SHURIKENJITSU

You begin the adventure with three 'Shuriken'. Normally, you carry five but you have lost two on your adventures. The type you specialise in are 'throwing stars', small razor-sharp star-shaped disks of metal. You can throw these up to a range of about thirty feet with devastating effect. If you throw a Shuriken, you will be given a Defence number for your target. Roll two dice, and if the score is higher than the Defence number, you will have hit your target. If this is the case, roll one die. The score is the amount of damage the Shuriken does. Subtract it from your target's Endurance. You may find yourself in a position where you are unable to retrieve a Shuriken once you have thrown it. Keep a running total in the box provided on your Character Sheet, crossing off a Shuriken each time you lose one. If you have none left, you can no longer use this skill.

ARROW CUTTING

Requiring excellent muscular co-ordination, hand and eye judgement and reflexes, this skill will enable you to knock aside, or even catch, incoming missiles such as arrows or spears.

ACROBATICS

The ability to leap and jump using flips, cartwheels, etc. like a tumbler or gymnast.

IMMUNITY TO POISONS

This involves taking small doses of virulent poisons over long periods of time, slowly building up the body's resistance. This enables the Ninja to survive most poison attempts.

FEIGNING DEATH

Requiring long and arduous training, a Ninja with this ability is able to slow down his heart rate and metabolism through will power alone, thus appearing to be dead.

ESCAPOLOGY

A Ninja with this skill is able to dislocate the joints of the body and to maximise the body's suppleness, allowing movement through small spaces, and escape from bonds and chains by slipping out of them.

POISON NEEDLES

Sometimes known as spitting needles, a Ninja with this skill can place small darts, coated with a powerful poison that acts in the blood stream, onto his tongue. By curling the tongue into an 'O' shape and spitting or blowing, the dart can be propelled up to an effective range of about fifteen feet. A useful surprise attack, the source of which is not always perceptible.

PICKING LOCKS, DETECTING AND DISARMING TRAPS

The ability to open locked doors, chests etc. A Ninja with this skill would carry various lockpicks in the pockets of his costume, including a small crowbar or jemmy. You are also trained to notice traps and to use the lock-picking tools to disarm them.

CLIMBING

Comprehensive training in the use of a Grappling Hook and hand and foot clamps, or Cat's Claws. The padded four-pronged hook has forty feet of rope attached to it and is used to hook over walls, niches etc., allowing the Ninja to pull himself up the rope. The Cat's Claws are spiked clamps, worn over the palm of the hand and the instep of the feet, enabling the Ninja to embed his Claws into a wall and climb straight up like a fly, and even to crawl across ceilings.

NINJA TOOLS

As well as any equipment you may take depending on your skills, as a Ninja you will have certain tools with you from the beginning. These are:

THE NINJA COSTUME

During the day you would normally be disguised as a traveller, beggar or suchlike. At night, when on a mission, you would wear costume. This consists of a few pieces of black cloth. One piece is worn as a jacket covering the chest and arms, two others are wound around each leg and held in at the waist. Finally, a long piece of cloth is wrapped around the head, leaving only the eyes exposed. The reverse side of the costume can be white, for travel over snowy ground, or green, for travel in woods or grasslands.

IRON SLEEVES

Sewn into the sleeves of your costume are four thin

strips of iron, the length of your forearm. These allow you to parry or block blows from swords and other cutting weapons.

BREATHING TUBE

Made from bamboo, this can be used as a snorkel allowing you to remain under water for long periods of time. It can also be used as a blow-pipe in conjunction with the Poison Needles skill, for added range.

GAROTTE

A specialised killing tool of the Ninja, this is a length of wire used to assassinate enemies by strangulation.

FLASH POWDER

This powder, when thrown in any source of flame, causes a blinding flash. Usually you carry enough for one use only, but you have already used your powder. You will have to wait until you can obtain some more.

FLINT AND TINDER

Used for making fires.

SPIDERFISH

Salted and cured, this highly venomous fish is used as a source for the deadly poison used in conjunction with the Poison Needles skill, and as a useful way of removing any guardian beasts.

THE BLOOD OF NIL

You usually carry one dose of the most virulent poison known on Orb but you have already used it to kill Honoric. This venom is extremely difficult and very dangerous to collect for it is taken from the barb of a scorpion son of the god, Nil, Mouth of the Void.

SPECIAL RULES FOR BOOK 2

If you have not played and successfully completed Book 1 – AVENGER! – in the Way of the Tiger series then you begin this book with the equipment listed. If you have successfully completed Book 1, then you should continue ASSASSIN! with the same character. Simply transfer all the information on your original Character Sheet to the one given in Book 2. You will begin with the number of Shuriken you had left in Book 1 but your Endurance and Inner Force scores have been restored to maximum by your god, Kwon. You have also learned one new skill from the existing list of eight. Add the one you have chosen to your Character Sheet. You also continue Book 2 with any special items you may have picked up on your journey to Quench-heart Keep. Most importantly, you should transfer all your Modifiers (Fate, Punch, Kick and Throw) to your new Character Sheet and the knowledge of Kwon's Flail, if you learnt that skill in Book 1.

With these skills and weapons at your disposal you are now a Ninja warrior and ready to take a step in **The Way of the Tiger**. Now turn to **1**.

1

From the echoing footfalls you guess that more than twenty soldiers are running up the Keep's spiral staircase towards you and they will surely try to kill you when they find out what you have done to their leader, Honoric, and his allies, Yaemon and Manse the Deathmage. The roof is still dimly lit by the glowing coals from a brazier. Will you:

Defend the top of the staircase, so that they can only come at you singly (turn to 17)?

Try an enormous leap from the Keep's roof, hoping that you can clear the castle wall and land in the moat far below (turn to 34)?

If you are skilled at Climbing, you may wish to climb down the outside wall of the Great Keep (turn to 52)?

2

Your tiger-like speed carries you beyond the falling grille which slams into the stone floor with a crack. Breathing a sigh of relief, you return to the main tunnel and continue on into the mountain. Turn to 76.

3

You are now hopelessly lost and uncertain whether, in the darkness and the confusion of flight, you may have missed a tunnel which leads out of the mountain. The stairs lead upwards for what seems like an age and at last bring you to a cross-roads. Gritting your teeth in tired determination you opt for the opposite tunnel which continues upwards. At last you see a welcoming circle of daylight ahead and your footsteps quicken without your even realising as you smell the beautiful fresh air. When you emerge you are high up on the far side of the mountains from Quench-heart Keep, and a great panorama of forests and wild lands rolls below you towards the valley of the Crow river in the far west. Turn to **235**.

4

You have time to pluck it out and recognise the familiar acrid smell of Spiderfish venom before your body jerks uncontrollably, and you are racked by painful spasms. Within moments the venom has reached your heart and it stops forever. Yaemon has been avenged.

5

The magician surrenders his ring to the swordsman and Thybault turns to you to ask if there is anything he can do to reward you for saving them. If you are wounded he heals you and you regain any lost points of Endurance. If you came through the caves of the goblins he notices swellings on your body and tells you that you have caught the plague. Praying to Avatar, he lays his hand on your forehead and drains the sickness from you. This done they leave the hill-top, walking east towards the Sea of the Star. You take your leave of them, anxious to reach a port where you may take ship to the Island of Tranquil Dreams. Will you head south-west, a way that looks rough and woody (turn to **44**), or due west where the land is more open and there is less cover (turn to **32**)?

6

The city is large and flourishing but a surprising number of young urchins, almost without clothes, run about the streets in gangs. You notice that they are adept at keeping out of people's way. As you walk briskly through the busy streets hoping to find a tavern where you may learn about ports on the Endless Sea, a sudden flare of light catches your eye. A wizened old woman bends over a battered cart which has lost its wheels and been turned upside down to serve as a shop counter. On the boards lie a great many unusual things; some which she claims to be the internal organs of exotic beasts such as chimaerae or hippogriffs, useful in magical rites, look more like sheep's offal to you, but the sudden flaring of light is unmistakable. The old witch is selling Flash Powder at five gold pieces a bag. If you have enough gold and wish to buy some you may do so. As you examine her wares further, a sudden tornado seems to start up around you, scattering the old crone's curiosities, and coloured lights explode before your eyes, leaving you momentarily stunned. You recover in a few moments and you feel inside the leather jerkin which you now wear. The Scrolls of Kettsuin are gone. Whirling about, you see a tall man with very curly hair dyed a bright corn yellow, contrasting with the shadowy sable cloak which he wears, walking away through the crowd. They seem to melt away from him. He is far from inconspicuous and you follow at a run, but he disappears suddenly. He has turned invisible. Your keen huntsman's hearing picks up the sounds of his footsteps as he moves down a back alley at a run, and you follow. Turn to **43**.

7

You bed down for the night under a stand of yew trees. Make a Fate Roll. If Fate smiles on you, turn to **35**. If Fate turns her back on you, turn to **307**.

8

Taking the Water Crystal which the prince of the Sea-Elves gave to you for helping to save him from the Sea-Jackals, you cast it to the floor at your feet. It shatters leaving a small blue drop on the damp floor which swells until a huge watery figure, like a breaking wave, towers above you. You order it to protect you and it turns on your adversaries. Cassandra backs to the oak-panelled door which she bolted behind you and Tyutchev takes several paces backwards as well. Thaum begins a spell. He is too far away to attack, but if you have a Shuriken left you may try to throw one. If you have none, turn to **20**. If you do have one, make a Shuriken Roll. Thaum's Defence as he concentrates on his spell is only 4. If you hit him turn to **31**. If not, your throwing star flies harmlessly into the wall; turn to **20**.

9

The night passes uneventfully but when you awake in the morning you find yourself in the grip of a raging fever. Large black swellings cover your body and you drift into a delirium in which you dream that you are helpless, outside the gates of the Temple of the Rock, on the Island of Tranquil Dreams, and surrounded by all the foes you have killed. When the sun is high in the sky, awareness returns as Thybault lays his hand upon your brow and, praying to Avatar, begins a chant. As he chants, the plague which you caught in the goblin caves is drawn from you and you are left weakened but cured. Taflwr examines your body for wounds and cures any that he finds. You regain any points of Endurance you have lost. The adventurers keep watch over you for another night, until your strength returns and you ask them about the lands which lie between you and the Endless Sea. They tell you that the lands and mountains to the south are peopled by dwarves, who are suspicious of men and inhospitable. The way south-west leads through a rough country where brigands often ambush helpless travellers. To the west, the land is open, giving little cover. In any case, they say, all paths lead to the city of Harith, on the Crow river and you are bound to come there on your way to the shores of the Endless Sea. When you are ready to go on your way, you thank them for their help and set off through the hills. Will you travel west (turn to 32) or south-west (turn to 44)?

10

You ease yourself off the roof and swing to the pillared cloister of the boardwalk by the red and black lacquered doors. Everything is quiet, save for the crickets and the rustle of the trees as a night breeze blows up. Suddenly the doors open and you are face to face with a figure, startling in its similarity to your own. He is dressed as you save for the curved, scabbarded sword or Ninjato strapped to his back and crouches in an attitude of quiet stealth. The black eyes, glittering in the moonlight through the slit of his wrap-around hood, widen in surprise; he did not expect to see you here. He reacts instinctively, leaping back and slamming the doors. But you are ready for this and leap into the air delivering a flying Winged Horse kick, smashing the doors aside with a resounding crash. He is halfway across the room, and he whirls with a curse, just as your hand blurs, sending a Shuriken flying towards him. Make a Shuriken Roll. His Defence is 7. If you are successful, turn to **410**. If you fail, turn to **24**.

11

The *Winged Serpent* will sail no further south on this

trip. You will have to travel across the Island of Plenty to the southern port of Iga and take ship there for your homeland, the Island of Tranquil Dreams. Hardred's messenger sets out to tell certain 'safe' people of your arrival and later you accompany him to the home of a wealthy aristocrat, the widow of a local daimio. On your way you pass a group of men, Samurai warriors, resplendent in red armour made of slats of lacquered wood. They carry long, curved swords, katana, with which they can cut through a man's neck like a knife through honey. The messenger tells you that they serve the great Daimio, or Lord, Kiyamo. You are graciously received by Singing Wind, in her beautiful house on the highest of Lemné's seven hills. You are enjoying the ceremony of the taking of tea with her when a messenger arrives. He bears a rod of ivory carrying the seal of Kiyamo, and he entreats you to travel to the daimio's palace saying that the Island of Tranquil Dreams is in danger. The thought of returning home to find the island pillaged and despoiled horrifies you and you respectfully take your leave of Singing Wind and set off towards Kiyamo's palace. Turn to **91**.

12

The grappling hook slides too far along the tunnel floor and the grille slams down, trapping you. After a fruitless hour in which you try to break the iron bars, you are discovered by goblins who live in the caves. Hundreds of them, cackling gleefully, carry water to the top of the spiral tunnel in whatever soiled vessels they can lay their hands on. The level of the water rises and you are forced to appeal to Kwon the Redeemer to be your salvation. Turn to **95**.

13

With both hands, your opponent cuts straight down at your head, the blade a blur, its tip arcing from a point near the small of his back to the top of your head. In an instant you clap your hands together inches above your head, trapping the blade, a feat of extraordinary judgement and co-ordination. Still holding the blade you jump and drive the ball of your foot at the Ninja's throat with a cry, and thus effect a Leaping Tiger kick. It smashes into his throat; his arms fly up and he sails backwards to crash in a heap, the blow killing him instantly. You are left, the blade still in your hands – the victor – in the silent empty house. Exhausted, you sleep where you are, a deep sleep haunted by gliding black shapes that seem intent on killing you. But you wake somewhat refreshed. Gain 3 Endurance. You may retrieve any Shuriken you have used before you set off to Kiyamo's palace. Turn to **168**.

14

You remember the Dancing Sword which is of no use to you, but obviously very magical. Pulling it out you show the adventurers, and the swordsman's eyes light up. He wears a grey surcoat with an unfurled scroll emblazoned across his chest, a symbol which holds no significance to you. He asks to look at it and you sense that it is safe to let him hold it. His brows furrow in concentration and he murmurs quietly until the sword leaps from his hands into the air, ready to do his bidding. The adventurers exclaim out loud. This is a sword of wondrous power, but it needs a command of the magic language used on spell-casting scrolls in order for it to be usable. Taflwr, of the Illustran priesthood, suggests to Eris that he give you the Sun-Star ring so that Vespers can keep the sword. Eris protests but

Thybault adds the weight of his argument to Taflwr's and, at length, he gives you the Sun-Star jewel. He tells you that if you speak the word 'Rahelios' a Sun-Star will burst from the ring and explode with great power. Thybault adds that it is useful to point the ring at one's enemies rather than at oneself. As night approaches you decide to go down with them from the barrow-hill, and take your turn at keeping night watch. Turn to **9**.

15

As you sit cross-legged, musing on the ways of the world, you catch sight of the bald head of one of the monks. He rounds a large magnolia tree and walks towards you, smiling a greeting. It is Hardred, the Grandmaster of the Temple to Kwon. 'A ship?' you ask hopefully. Hardred nods and reaches inside his brown habit. Your acute senses immediately detect danger. This is not Hardred at all; more likely it is Mandrake. Turn to **382**.

16

You pluck the needle out and recognise the acrid smell of Spiderfish venom before you look up to see the blade of a curved sword splitting the wall open. You leap to your feet, but your body betrays you and you are overcome by dizziness and nausea, as you begin to overcome the effects of the poison. Your vision clears in time to see a figure, clad in black from head to toe, with only his eyes showing through a wrap-around hood, wielding a wickedly curved sword. With lightning speed he passes it across your throat. Death is instantaneous.

17

You wait at the top of the torch-lit staircase and the first of the mail-clad soldiers surges around the corner towards you. He is one of the Keep guards and carries a long sword and a black shield with the symbol of the Sword of Doom on it which he throws upwards as he jabs at your midriff. Will you try to throw him down the stairs, using the Dragon's Tail throw (turn to **70**), try to knock him down with an Iron Fist punch (turn to **85**), or use the Winged Horse kick (turn to **101**)?

18

Your tiger-like speed falters due to the fatigue which numbs your body. You are too slow and the barbed grille slams into your belly and lodges in your back-bone. You suffer an agonising and slow death deep within the Goblin's Teeth Mountains.

19

The man grins at you like an imbecile and his head lolls to one side, as if his neck had no spine. He slobbers as he asks you if you would like to have a look at his white dragon's egg which he found in an ice-cave in the snow wastes. He points at the odd-shaped bundle. Will you humour him by looking in the bundle (turn to **49**), attack him (turn to **56**) or pat him on the head and walk on (turn to **64**)?

20

Thaum's spell is finished and a small ball of flame leaves his hand, growing as it streaks towards the

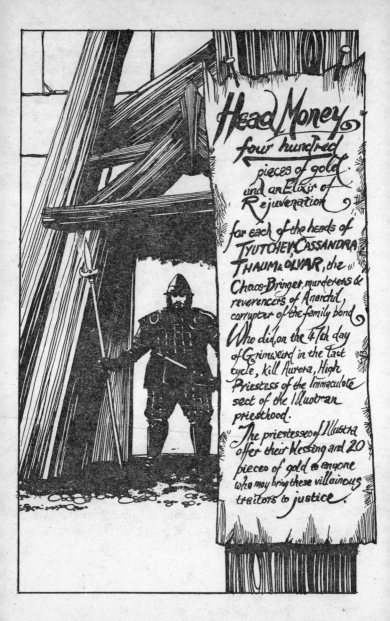

Head Money

four hundred pieces of gold. and an Elixir of Rejuvenation

for each of the heads of TYUTCHEV, CASSANDRA, THAUM & OLVAR, the Chaos-Bringer, murderers & reverencers of Anarchil, corrupter of the family bond

Who did, on the 47th day of Grimweird in the last cycle, kill Aurora, High Priestess of the Immaculate sect of the Illustran priesthood.

The priestesses of Illustra offer their blessing and 20 pieces of gold to anyone who may bring these villainous traitors to justice.

water elemental which now towers above him. There is an explosion and a huge fireball erupts around the elemental just as it is about to crash down on the magician like a tidal wave. A pillar of steam rises up and spreads beneath the ceiling; your elemental has been banished to its home on the elemental plane of water by Thaum's potent thaumaturgy. Cassandra and Tyutchev close in once more. You step back and attack the warrior woman. Turn to **121**.

21

You walk on and, towards the end of the day, enter the valley of the Crow river. The meadows are full of asphodel and roses. You make your way down towards the large river, which flows west, towards the Endless Sea. The fertile land at the edge of the river is strip-farmed; each peasant pays a part of his crop to his lord for the right to a thin strip of land, in some cases only five yards across. You purloin the breeches and jerkin of a peasant which you find lying on a rock to dry in the sun. Then you walk briskly along the towpath towards the city of Harith, to join the influx of farmers seeking the safety or excitement of the city at the end of the day's toil. At the great gate, a single guard in black armour stands stock still, impassive in the centre of the street. He bears no token to give a clue as to which god he serves, but he lets you pass. Beyond the gate is a small stone building which flies the green and white flag. Your professional interest is aroused by a piece of weathered parchment nailed to a board outside:

HEAD MONEY

Four hundred pieces of gold and an Elixir of Rejuvenation for each of the heads of TYUTCHEV, CASSANDRA, THAUM and OLVAR the CHAOS-BRINGER, murderers and reverencers of Anarchil, corrupter of the family bond. Who did, on the forty-seventh day of Grimweird in the last cycle, kill Aurora, High Priestess of the immaculate sect of the Illustran priesthood.

The priestesses of Illustra offer their blessing and twenty pieces of gold to anyone who may bring these villainous traitors to justice.

You pause in thought and then remember that you killed a barbarian warrior who called himself Olvar the Chaos-Bringer in Fortune Pass on the way to Quench-heart Keep. If you would like to enter the building, turn to **60**. If you prefer to pass by, turn to **6**.

22

Your opponent speaks, his voice flat and emotionless. 'I am Ninja. I follow the Way of the Scorpion. I have slain all your guards and I shall slay you, thus proving that the Way of the Scorpion overshadows the Way of the Tiger, just as the power of Nemesis overshadows the power of Kwon.' With that he launches into a devastating attack, his sword a blur as it flashes through the air. You must try to block it. Your Defence is 7. If you succeed, turn to **335**. If you fail, turn to **354**.

23

You swim further from the shore, hoping that your pursuers will lose sight of you, when the water around you becomes strangely calm. You swim on

until something seems to pull at your body and you are carried into the eye of a whirlpool. You are helpless as it sucks you into its eye and then fathoms downward into the green depths. Try as you might you cannot escape and you resign yourself to holding your breath. As you are whirled ever deeper a blue-skinned merman swims past, as if fleeing, but seeing you he cups his hands and a globe of air forms in the sea which drifts towards you. Your head is soon inside it. Miraculously, you can breathe again. The merman speaks and you hear him in your mind, 'The jackals of the sea have kidnapped the prince of the Sea-Elves. You are being carried to their coral meadows. Do not fear the horned whale.' With that he is gone with a grace and speed that no man could ever match. As you stare down through the maelstrom of tiny bubbles you see a great bed of red and purple coral lying below you. Turn to **41**.

24

Your Shuriken hurtles towards his throat and his eyes widen with astonishment but, with a shout, and in one incredibly swift motion he reaches up with both hands, draws his sword and knocks the Shuriken aside. There is the clear ring of steel on steel and a whirring hum as the Shuriken twists away, followed by a crisp tearing sound as it goes in and out through the paper-thin wall. There is a pause as you both stare at each other, the insistent flutter of shreds of the torn wall in a sudden night breeze echoing the flurry of explosive violence. He stands, presenting only the side of his body to you, right foot forward, left knee bent and at right angles to his body, sword-hip pointing up at your throat, arms extended. You begin to circle each other warily. Turn to **22**.

25

The adventurers eye you warily, but give freely of their food: dried meat and oatmeal biscuits. You recognise the second priest to be a follower of the goddess Illustra, goddess of Life, Consort to Avatar, the Supreme Principle of Goodness. The priest in white, who tells you his name is Thybault, begins to criticise the young magician.

'In the name of all that is good, Eris, what demon possessed you that you should cast the Noisome Vapours around a being that does not need to draw breath to exist? If not for our saviour here we would have joined the wraith in its barrow by now. It's a fine magician who cannot even dispel his own magicks.'

Eris blushes and turns away, but the swordsman, Vespers, moans: 'My sword-arm will never be what it was. I said that we should not have taken up with the worshipper of a Chaos god.' Eris begins to laugh as you accept some food. The second priest whose name is Taflwr and wears a white cross on green and follows the Goddess Illustra, says that he knows that Eris made no more than a simple mistake, but he suggests the magician give Vespers his Sun-Star ring as the swordsman's sword-arm is crippled beyond magical healing. If you have the Goblin King's Dancing Sword, turn to **14**. If not turn to **5**.

26

The grappling hook jams underneath the barbed grille and you are able to slide beneath it, on your back. You manage to drag the hook out from under the grille which then slams to the floor with a crash. You rejoin the main tunnel and continue on into the mountain. Turn to **76**.

27

You lie back, putting your recent nightmares out of your mind, and quickly fall asleep. But soon your heightened sense of hearing wakens you again. There is a faint scraping noise in the room. You sit up and look around but can see nothing in the candlelight. A slight movement catches your eye. A thin bamboo tube pokes its way through a small hole in the thin wall of your room and, before your eyes can even widen in surprise, there is a faint woosh and a small feathered needle has embedded itself in your shoulder. Do you have Immunity to Poisons? If you do, turn to **16**. If you do not, turn to **4**.

28

The torturer returns, his head heavily bandaged but still wearing his black leather executioner's hood. You cannot see his expression as he examines your bonds and pronounces that he is satisfied with the handywork of the guards. When they have told him that you have killed Yaemon, Honoric and Manse the Deathmage his voice fills with false anger. 'I can see my ingenuity will be stretched to the limit thinking up fitting punishments for you, Ninja.' He orders the guards from the chamber and turns to examine the manacles in a small furnace. Using your skill as an Escapologist you dislocate one arm and by tensing certain muscles and inching your steel-like fingers between the bonds, you struggle free. Mercifully, the boy remains silent as you creep like a stalking tiger towards the broad, sweating back of the torturer. With a cry you explode into a kick which sends his head flying into the furnace. The boy cheers weakly as you close the furnace door on the neck of the sadistic torturer, muffling his death agonies. You free the prisoners and the boy tells you that there is a way of escape through the underground river which connects the pool in this chamber to the moat. Knowing that you must restore the Scrolls of Kettsuin to safety, you thank him and dive in. Turn to **153**.

29

From behind a tree you watch the O-Bakemono at work. After a while the huge lumbering creature stops breaking up wood and, gathering a mass of logs in its huge arms, it shuffles up to the rock-face and growls at it. You can just make out the word 'Baal'. There is a rumble and a slab of stone swings outward from the rock and the O-Bakemono shuffles into the darkness beyond, the door closing behind it. You wait a half hour and then step to the rock-face. Beside the tracks of the O-Bakemono you can also see that the grass has been scorched, and fluted grooves some two feet wide have been left in the earth, as if something heavy and tubular had been dragged along it, disappearing into the rock-face. You speak the word and the rock opens again. A cave mouth yawns before you. You walk into it and it narrows to a winding corridor lit with torches. Eventually, the tunnel opens out into a large cavern with a huge fire in the middle. On the far wall is a crude altar stained with ominous black patches and adorned with black candles and a hideous idol, a few feet in height, of a creature half man, half insect. In the corner lies a pile of material and the possessions of the villagers that are of any worth. Just ahead of you is a young girl, the farmer's daughter, chained to a stake near the fire, her face streaked with tears and the dirt of the cavern. Nearest you, and with its back to you, sits the O-Bakemono, chewing on a raw goat's leg. But, rearing up before the girl and taunting her cruelly, is the worst and most incredible sight of all: an enormous twenty foot serpent with coils at least two feet wide, and with the torso of a human woman. Her eyes are green and luminous, her face twisted and evil and framed with long tangled black hair; she has fanged teeth protruding from red lips – she is the Hannya, a witch who worships a Demonlord and in return is given the body of a serpent. Just then the O-Bakemono stops gnawing its meat and sniffs the air. It has caught your scent. Will you:

Steal in, hugging the shadows and then dash out and try to Garotte the beast (turn to 51)?

Creep in and spit a Poison Needle at the O-Bakemono, if you have that skill (turn to 71)?

Creep in and, if you have played AVENGER! and learnt this kick, use Kwon's Flail with Inner Force (if you have any left) on the O-Bakemono (turn to 398)?

Or daub the venom of the Spiderfish on Cassandra's dagger (if you have it), creep in and stab the O-Bakemono (turn to 180)?

30

You cannot defeat the undead Barbarian by taking the life which it gave up many centuries ago. Your blows which would maim a normal man merely break off parts of the undead Warlord's body without halting its onslaught. Halve any damage which your blows cause. You must dismember it entirely if the arcane magic which gave it life is to be dispelled. If you have just punched this foe turn to 86 and read on, from the attack of the undead Warlord. If you have just kicked it, turn to 74 and read on from the Warlord's attack.

31

Your throwing star whirrs from your hand and embeds itself in the magician's chest and he crumples to the damp floor of the cellar, his spell lost. The water elemental breaks on him like a tidal wave and he is thrown against the wall with a force that stoves in his chest and leaves him lifeless on the floor. The water elemental seems to drain away into the rock, but then the left hand wall of the cellar caves in with a thunder-clap and dust fills the room. Turn to **413**.

32

You strike out across open grasslands, bare but for occasional giant pine trees which seem almost to stir the clouds with their tips as they sway creaking in the wind. You walk from dawn to dusk for two days. Your sleep does little more than restore you from the fatigue which you feel each sundown. As evening approaches on the third day, you see a shaven-headed man in a sandy brown robe, sitting on a flat rock, close to the path along which you are travelling. He has a bundle of sacking at his side. If you decide to break into a run and give him a wide berth, turn to **7**. If you decide instead to walk up and greet him, turn to **19**.

33

Each day you pace the shoreline, looking out to sea at the ships which row into the harbour. Your heart yearns for the Island of Tranquil Dreams and the safe fulfilment of your mission. The family with whom you are lodging do not trouble you and you say little, keeping yourself to yourself. At last, a large three-masted, square-sailed ship anchors off the sandy beach. A messenger bids you be ready to sail on the morrow; the ship is preparing to set sail once more for Upanishad, a great city far to the south. Turn to **406**.

34

You sprint across the rain-puddled roof of the Great Keep and launch yourself into the night air. You will have to travel forty feet from the rooftop if you are to clear the castle wall and land safely in the moat. Make a Fate Roll. If Fate smiles on you, turn to **383**. If Fate turns her back on you, turn to **401**.

35

Something has startled you awake – anyone who lacked the senses of a hunting tiger would have heard nothing, but a rustling alerts you to some-thing moving on your right. You move soundlessly to your feet but cannot see anything. You pass the night vigilantly awake and when, in the morning, you embark again on your journey to the Endless Sea, you are intrigued to see the man in the sandy brown robe sitting on the ground beside your path. At his side is the bundle of sacking which he had beside him yesterday. The man grins at you like an imbecile and his head lolls to one side, as if his neck had no spine. He slobbers as he asks you if you would like to have a look at his White Dragon's egg which he found in an ice-cave in the Snow Wastes.

He points at the odd-shaped bundle. Will you humour him by looking in the bundle (turn to **49**), attack him (turn to **56**), or pat him on the head and walk on (turn to **64**)?

(turn to **49**), (turn to **56**), (turn to **64**)

36

They thank you and say that they will pray that you get through to the palace. You promise them that the soldiers will be here within the day and, eating a hurried meal, jog on up the mountain road to the palace. You leave the road and stealthily pick your way through the wooded mountainside, leaving no trace of your passage. Some way on, you rejoin the road unmolested. The road winds up the mountain, a sheer drop on one side. As evening approaches you round the corner and sight the palace of Lord Kiyamo. It lies in a shallow valley between two peaks, surrounded by magnificent ornamental gardens and a high stone wall punctuated by tall watchtowers. The Main Gate is hung with banners, emblazoned with the Mons of Kiyamo, glittering in the sun.

You approach the guards at the gate and hand them the ivory token. Without a word, they lead you through the gates, past the large open area where Samurai and other soldiers are practising their swordsmanship and archery and on into the ornamental gardens. Presently, you are led into a richly furnished Reception Hall where you are asked politely to wait. Your guards bow and leave you. Presently a man in white robes adorned with stylised flowers of deep ultramarine comes into the hall. He has two swords, one long and the other short, tucked into a sash at his waist. He introduces himself as Onikaba, Kiyamo's chief adviser and tells you he has recently returned from the Island of

Tranquil Dreams where he has talked much with the Grandmaster of the Dawn. It seems they know of your success in retrieving the Scrolls of Kettsuin and pray to Kwon for your safe return.

He leads you into a long chamber of polished wood where Lord Kiyamo sits cross-legged in front of a low table, covered in scrolls and maps. Armed Samurai line the walls. He motions for you to sit beside him and tea is served. He is a man in middle years, his shoulders and arms heavy with muscle from repeated practice with the sword. Turn to **66**.

37

The undead Warlord is no more than a shredded mound of grotesque decay. The dark light in its eyes has gone and the blade of its sword turns to smoke before your eyes. A sudden breeze gets up, wafting the yellow gas away from the hilltop and you look around. The swordsman lies bleeding on the ground. The men in white and green, priests you guess, although one was wearing armour, are not badly wounded and are overcoming the sickness caused by the magician's spell. The magician himself seems glad to see them alive, but looks sheepishly at the ground. The priest in green lays his hands upon the swordsman who seems to recover a little, whilst the priest in white turns to face you. 'Well, thank you my friend, you have saved our lives, but how was it that you could breathe inside the yellow cloud?'

'He looks like an assassin to me,' says the young magician pointing at you as the swordsman rises to his feet. 'Well at any rate I thank you, in the name of Avatar, the Supreme Principle of Good for ridding Orb of this evil.'

Despite the fact that their recent performance suggests otherwise you judge them powerful adventurers, hardened in the wilderness of Orb. Will you accept the priest of Avatar's invitation to eat with them (turn to 25) or vanish down the hillside as suddenly as you came (turn to 172)?

38

Hatemoto Hizen and six Samurai lead you through the ornamental gardens to the guest house in the palace grounds. You cross a tranquil pond, covered in white lilies, and pass through a sweet smelling glade filled with flowering plants and trees arranged carefully, giving an effect of ordered beauty. The setting sun bathes the gardens of the palace in deep crimson light. A feeling of peace and calm comes over you. Presently, you follow a stone path that winds between two stone lanterns to the red and black lacquered double doors of the guest house. It is a pagoda-like structure with a tiled roof and paper-thin walls. Hizen leads you through the doors into a lavishly furnished room, with ornately carved chests, wall hangings and screens adorned with simple water-colour paintings of birds, flowers and landscapes. You follow him through a sliding door into an inner courtyard, where a fountain tinkles quietly into a basin that overflows into a stone pool. Looking up, you see the moon rising.

Hizen goes on through another sliding door on the left into a larger room where a long, low table is laden with steaming bowls of rice, crisp fried vegetables and strips of marinated raw fish. Suddenly you realise how hungry you are and you sit cross-legged, your back to two sliding doors, on a tatami, or mat, to eat. Hizen sits with you and tells you that three of the Samurai will be on guard outside the guest house at all times, one on patrol, the others at the front and back of the house. 'Rest and recuperate, Ninja,' he says. Indeed, you are tired after your long ordeal. A young girl, in white robes, serves tea and retires to a kitchen, through one of the three sliding doors in the room. Ahead of you there is an alcove, in which rests a print of a Samurai warrior slaying a large winged and clawed serpent. After you have eaten, Hizen shows you to a room beside the kitchen, lit by an hour candle, where a steaming bath and a futon (or mattress) are waiting for you. He departs, wishing you a good night's sleep. Turn to **50**.

39

Only the cat-like speed of your reactions can save you from being trapped. Roll two dice:

If you score 4 or more, turn to **2**.
If you score 3 or less, turn to **18**.

40

You edge around the clearing until you are behind the scaly humanoid and silently glide across the open ground until you are close enough. With a shout you leap into the air and slam into the creature's back, wrapping your Garotte around its throat in an iron grip, a thin red line already appearing where the wire bites deep. However the O-Bakemono is much stronger than you thought possible. It has not moved more than an inch, despite your added weight, nor does it seem troubled by the Garotte. It simply reaches behind its back and lifts, dashing you to the ground before it with a roar. You roll with the fall but the force of the throw was such that you still lose 3 Endurance; your body is battered and bruised. You leap to your feet and slowly back off to the edge of the clearing. The O-Bakemono seems to have a very limited intelligence. It simply glares at you and then continues to break up wood. It would appear to obey the commands of its mistress to the letter. Will you go back into the trees and hide, watching to see what happens next (turn to 29), use a Poisoned Needle on the beast, if you have that skill (turn to 185) or run and use Kwon's Flail and Inner Force, if you have played AVENGER! and learnt that kick, *and* have some Inner Force left (turn to 171)?

41

You are thrown free at the base of the whirlpool towards a fan-shaped piece of white coral called Dead Men's Fingers which you know to be deadly poisonous. The globe of air allows you to breathe freely. Will you examine the fan-shaped coral (turn to 68), swim in search of the prince of the Sea-Elves (turn to 81) or swim back to the surface (turn to 97)?

42

You run from the temple and your uncanny sense of direction allows you to find your way back to the underground gate which leads to the gardens of the monastery. Confident that you have not been followed you seek Hardred, only to be told that he has gone to the harbour to make enquiries about ships sailing south, on your behalf. At length you decide to await his return, and settle under the shade of the plane tree once more. Turn to 15.

The tall thief's footprints in the dust show you the way he has passed through the maze of back streets, and you can hear him panting lightly as a great stone edifice comes into view before you. He runs towards its forbidding bulk and you see that it is a great church with tall circular towers, around the outside of which spiral staircases twine like great serpents. Snake-head gargoyles with gaping mouths threaten the streets below. You see the door to a stable move slightly and you dart in, past the whinnying horses, where you are in time to see a trap-door shutting behind some sheaves of barley-stalks. You leap over the straw and listen carefully at the trap-door. The sound of two sets of receding footsteps suggests it is safe to open the door and you drop down to a damp stone stairway below.

The stairs lead downwards and in the direction of the forbidding church. Narrow shafts lead up to sky-lights at intervals and the man you are silently following becomes visible once more, running beside a man in a flowing grey robe. They run out into a large ill-lit cellar and around a corner. You follow stealthily until the sound of a door slamming shut and a bolt driven home stops you in your tracks. Looking round you see an unusually handsome young woman dressed in a bizarre patchwork of armour; her face is hard and she looks contemptuous. She has shut and barred a heavy oak door across the bottom of the damp staircase. It seems that rather than fleeing from you she has trapped you. 'Your fame is spreading across the land, Ninja. It is a shame for you that you met a friend of ours in Fortune Pass, Olvar, a kind and gentle barbarian from the northern lands.' She smiles as the two men whom you had been chasing step into sight at the other end of the cellar. The tall thief with the yellow

hair stands beside a magician who bears cabalistic signs on his flowing grey robes, and wears a large gold ear-ring in one ear. As you look into their callous eyes you feel that they could not summon up a drop of kindness between them. The woman tells you that her name is Cassandra. The others must be the men mentioned with her on the board near the gate – Tyutchev and Thaum – who with Olvar, the man you killed when he attacked you mindlessly in Fortune Pass, murdered Aurora, the high priestess at the cathedral to Illustra. Cassandra says that they are going to take their revenge for Olvar's death. Tyutchev draws a two-handed sword from behind his back as Cassandra bares her long sword.

Do you protest saying that you have never killed anyone in your life (turn to **82**), hurl a Shuriken if you have one, at one of them (turn to **108**), use some other item (turn to **147**) or attack Cassandra (turn to **121**)?

44

For two days you travel from dawn till dusk, gaining little rest. The hawthorn hedges and clumps of gorse mean that you must frequently go back on your tracks to find a way through. Your head is bowed in thought on this overcast day when a rustle of dried leaves catches your attention. You are walking down a narrow deer-path between hawthorn bushes, and three brigands with drawn swords are barring your onward path. There is no escape through the bushes and looking back you see three more move out from behind cover to trap you.

If you have the skill of Acrobatics you may wish to somersault over the three ahead of you and then attack them (turn to **57**). Or you may wish to use a

Shuriken if you have one (turn to **73**), or a Poison Needle if you are skilled with them (turn to **94**). If not you can only advance to attack the three you saw first (turn to **106**).

(turn to **73**) ... (turn to **94**) ... (turn to **106**)

45

Instead of a pass onto a trading ship Hardred produces a throwing dagger, which is flying to your heart before you can even recognise it for what it is. He throws too quickly for it to be Hardred. This is the last thought you have as the dagger pierces your heart. The blade is grooved and covered in venom, but the steel alone has done its work. As you die 'Hardred' bows and says 'Mandrake, Guildmaster of Assassins, at your service, Ninja. Honoric will be pleased.' You have failed.

46

The door opens onto a tunnel which bends downwards and sharply left. The air is musty and dank. The goblins are almost upon you and you decide to sprint down the tunnel. It turns, getting narrower and narrower, as it spirals down into the bones of the mountain, until you are suddenly faced with a dead end. You turn, but before you can race back up the tunnel a barbed metal grille slams from ceiling to floor, trapping you. The goblins stand on the other side gloating and cackling gleefully. After a while they leave you and a trickle of water reaches your feet. The water is being brought to the top of the tunnel by hundreds of goblins, in whatever soiled vessels they can find. There is no way out. The water level rises and all you can do is decide to call upon your god, Kwon the Redeemer, to save you. Turn to **95**.

47

You point the ring and shout the word 'Rahelios!' Who will you choose as your target: Cassandra (turn to **412**) or Thaum (turn to **418**)?

48

After a day's journey through the mountains, night has fallen and you are looking down on a myriad tiny lights – the camp of Jikkyu's army. You descend from the foothills and wend your stealthy way across the open fields, studded with wooded groves, towards the camp. You come to a line of perimeter sentry pickets, each marked by a fire some fifty yards apart, with two guards at each. Your night vision is excellent and you crawl soundlessly towards one, your black costume merging into the shadows of the night. You throw a stone onto the fire. A crack – the sentries glance for a moment at the fire and away again, their eyes momentarily blinded – and you glide past them like a ghost. Soon you are at the outer edge of an enormous expanse of tents. In the centre is a large dark pavilion unadorned save for a red flag fluttering at its top, almost certainly Jikkyu's tent. Crouching low, you make your way inward, avoiding the night patrols – some of which are squat and misshapen, long arms ending in talons – the Bakemono. Like a spectre you rise out of the night and catch a lone sentry with your Garotte, soundlessly choking the life out of him. Putting on his armour and weapons you walk openly to the large tent, unchallenged. Two guards stand at its front entrance which is well lit.

Will you creep round to the back of the tent, make a

small incision and look in (turn to **98**), try to kill the two guards as quickly and as quietly as possible (turn to **79**), or approach them, saying you are a messenger (turn to **387**)?

49

As you bend down and open the neck of the sack, the man rolls off the rock onto his back. As you turn to look, something leaps from the sack onto your head. It has claws which gouge into your neck and is like a purplish air-filled ball. It squashes itself against your face as you try to knock it away and you cannot see. You can feel a gristly stalk-like tube, however, which forces itself into your mouth as you open it to shout in pain and shock. As you bite on it, a stream of hot liquid shoots down your throat. If you have Immunity to Poisons, turn to **78**. If you have not, you realise, as your chest contracts in a spasm, that you have been poisoned. You are paralysed and the horrible bag-like thing flattens itself across your face so that you suffocate. The last thing you feel is the groping hands of the shaven-headed man as he searches you for the Scrolls of Kettsuin. You have failed.

50

The bath is invigorating and you feel refreshed and cleansed as you lie down on the futon to sleep, a pleasant fatigue stealing over you. Soon you are deep in sleep and dreaming. A vivid image comes into your mind. You are on a featureless expanse of nothingness. A tiger's head floats before you. Its fur is pure white and its eyes, completely blue, gaze serenely upon you, filling you with quiet strength and calm. Suddenly its mouth opens, revealing a gaping maw lined with many razor-sharp blood-stained teeth and it roars. A rushing wind blows forth, smothering you in a fetid, choking stench and another face grows out of the yawning blackness of the mouth, completely blotting out the white tiger's and its blue, blue eyes, still serene and somehow imbued with tranquility. Ahead of you now is the face of a Ninja, the black hood obscuring all features, save two black eyes, glinting malevolently. You wake with a start and as consciousness returns, you find yourself sitting bolt upright, bathed in sweat and breathing hard. The night is still and deathly quiet. The candle, still flickering, tells you that you have been asleep for about three hours. Will you return to sleep, knowing your tired body needs rest to recuperate (turn to **27**) or get up to talk to the guards (turn to **63**)?

51

You steal into the cavern as the O-Bakemono rises to its feet. Suddenly you burst out of the shadows and leap into the air and slam into the creature's back, wrapping your Garotte around its throat in an iron grip, a thin red line already appearing where the wire bites deep. However the O-Bakemono seems untroubled by the Garotte. It simply reaches behind its back and lifts, dashing you to the ground before it with a roar. You roll with the fall but before you can rise to your feet you are smothered beneath the coils of the Hannya – they are burning hot, like the fires of hell, and you are unable to move You are burnt, crushed and suffocated all at once.

52

You dart nimbly to the edge of the Keep's roof and, fixing your Cat's Claws to your wrists and hands, begin the difficult descent towards the grass of the Inner Bailey below. You can hear exclamations of horror from the guards above as they discover Yaemon's body but none of them thinks to look down the sheer sides of the Great Keep. You are half-way down before a break in the clouds allows the light of the moon to shine through. A guard in the Bailey sees what he takes to be a huge, black spider walking down the Keep wall and unleashes a crossbow bolt at you. Do you have the skill of Arrow Cutting? If you do, turn to **167**. If you do not, turn to **295**.

53

The undead Barbarian Warlord moves slowly and you decide to attempt the Teeth of the Tiger on the hulking wraith. You launch yourself feet first at the blank-faced head with its folds of purple flesh. Its eyes are pits of evil.

UNDEAD WARLORD
Defence against Teeth of the Tiger throw: 5
Endurance: 14
Damage: 1 Die + 2

If you throw the undead Warlord successfully you may add 2 to the die for your next attack and double any damage done as you strike at the rotted patch in its chest. If you fail, it drives its chill, gleaming sword at your groin. Your Defence as you try to roll aside is 7.

If it hits you, you must subtract 2 from your next two die rolls as a numbing cold slows your reactions. If you are still alive, you may kick (turn to **74**) or punch (turn to **86**).

54

You are in the Lap of Fate as the grille descends towards the tunnel floor. Roll one die:

If you score 1 or 6: turn to **26**.
If you score 2, 3, 4 or 5: turn to **12**.

55

You dart back, avoiding a wicked sword thrust, and then in, driving your foot at his abdomen and then up at his throat with lightning speed.

NINJA
Defence against Forked Lightning Strike kick: 7
Endurance: 19
Damage: 1 Die + 1

If you have reduced him to 0 or less Endurance, turn to **13**. If he still has Endurance, he cuts savagely at your extended leg. Your Defence against this is 7. If you survive the attack, will you try a Tiger's Paw chop (turn to **304**), a Whirlpool throw (turn to **87**) or kick again (return to the top of this paragraph)?

56

As you move to attack, the shaven-headed man chops his arm at your neck with the speed of a stooping hawk. You realise that he must be a martial arts monk. Your Defence against his sudden strike is 7. If you fail to dodge his blow he jars your body sickeningly. You lose 5 Endurance. If you survive his chop you may reply with a Dragon's Tail throw (turn to **125**), a Cobra Strike punch (turn to **142**) or a Forked Lightning Strike kick (turn to **169**).

57

Strangely, a pall of fear hangs over you but still you sprint forward and crouch, as if to punch at the leader's stomach, before launching yourself into an elegant piked somersault so that you land behind them and can attack before they realise what is happening. You may attack using the Tiger's Paw chop (turn to **140**), the Leaping Tiger kick (turn to **154**) or the Whirlpool throw (turn to **163**). Alternatively, you may run from this battle at any time. If you flee, turn to **201**.

58

The torturer is knocked backwards against the rack by your kicks but he rolls across the taut body of his prisoner, putting the rack between you as the guards run into the torture chamber behind you. You fight valiantly, knocking three of them unconscious with swift jabs and punches, but one of them catches you a lucky blow with his warhammer, knocking you to the floor. They pinion you and bind you with ropes and one of them begins heating a set of manacles in a small furnace while the torturer goes in search of bandages for his throbbing head. Are you a skilled Escapologist? If you are, turn to **28**. If you are not, turn to **344**.

59

Kwon cannot hear your forlorn cry; you are in the subterranean precincts of the temple to another god whose power here is too great to permit you salvation from another. Will you attack Cassandra before she spits you on her sword (turn to **121**) or use any item you may have picked up on your travels (turn to **147**)?

60

Three priestesses and a warrior guard, all dressed in green and white, stand up as you enter. The guard's sword hisses from its sheath, but one of the priestesses, a white-haired woman with bones so fine she looks elfin, welcomes you. You tell them that you killed a man named Olvar the Chaos-Bringer and describe him to them. The priestess looks interested:

'He wore a circlet which bore a blue gem on his forehead. Do you have it?' You shake your head and the priestess goes on. 'One northern barbarian looks very like another. If it was truly he we thank you, but we may not be so generous with the goddess's tribute as to give you reward-money without proof.' You decide to let it pass and ask about the other traitors mentioned on the board. The priestess presses her lips together, grim faced and says, 'They came to Harith, banished from Wargrave Abbas for similar atrocities. They worship the insane chaos god, Anarchil, and their only sport is wanton killing. They received the help of the temple to Anarchil here in the city and were audacious enough to desecrate our temple and kill the saintly Aurora in her own cathedral. Thaum is a master of illusion; through his trickery they escaped to the Manmarch. If what you say is true, I am surprised that you found Olvar alone; they were said to be inseparable. Perhaps the goddess has taken her revenge on the others. Would that it were so.'

You decide to leave now, before they can ask you what business brings you to Harith. Turn to **6**.

61

As you reach for a Shuriken Hardred produces a throwing dagger which is flying to your heart before you can even recognise it for what it is. He throws too quickly for it to be Hardred. If you have the skill of Arrow Cutting turn to **342**. If you do not, this is the last thought you have as the dagger pierces your heart. The blade is grooved and covered in venom, but the steel alone has done its work. As you die 'Hardred' bows and says 'Mandrake, Guildmaster of Assassins, at your service, Ninja. Honoric will be pleased.' You have failed.

62

Your aching limbs are charged with adrenalin as you launch yourself towards the goblin's body, knowing that if you should fail to reach it you will sink into the very being of the Primordial One. You sail above the heaving, black morass and your fingers cling onto the half-dissolved body of the goblin. As the nameless horror surges up towards you in a tidal wave of putrescent flesh you haul yourself up the plaited vine and set it to swing gently, untying the goblin's body as you do so, so that you can pull the bottom of the vine up out of the reach of the Primordial One. As the vine swings in an ever-greater arc, you catch sight of a flight of stone steps leading upwards beyond the goblins' god. Letting go, you somersault through the air and drop near the bottom step. As you look back the horror is feeding on the remains of the goblin, whose head is just disappearing below the heaving surface. Turn to **3**.

You get to your feet and don the costume of the Ninja before walking to the door and sliding it open. The eyes of the dying clawed-and-winged serpent seem to glare at you knowingly from the print opposite, the colours like shadows in the faint glow of your candle. You cross the room and, sliding open another door, step into the inner courtyard. The pool, rippling gently, reflects the pale light of the moon as it lends the cloudless night a ghostly luminescence. The air is filled with the rich scent of the ornamental gardens and the sound of insects and bullfrogs. It is warm and close; there is no breeze. Everything is quiet and peaceful but the night seems full of tense expectancy.

Silently, like a shade, you cross the courtyard, slide open the door, step in and slide it shut in one fluid motion. You are in almost complete darkness, in the first room of the guest house. You stand as still as a rock, your senses straining, reaching out into the almost tangible blackness ahead. Alarms seem to ring wildly in your head. But you find nothing. After a while you move on. By memory, you thread your way quietly through the furnishings to the front door, ears straining and spine tingling – you feel charged with nervous anticipation yet all seems still and you can sense nothing unusual in the room. You are about to open the door when for some reason you pause to listen, although you know all should be well here in the palace grounds of the only shogun for three hundred years. This must be the most heavily guarded place on all Lemné. You hear nothing save a leaden sigh of boredom. You pull the door open just a little and look out. One of the Samurai is leaning against a pillar, arms folded, humming to himself, as the patrolling Samurai continues around the house. You step out and he turns, a brief look of horror on his face as he sees your Ninja costume, before he smiles with greeting and not a little relief as he recognises you.

'What brings you out in the dawn hours, sir? Only the dead and poor unfortunate guards like myself walk at this hour!'

At this, you begin to feel foolish, and curse yourself for behaving like a frightened rabbit – you relax, like a taut bowstring that is unstrung. You tell the guard you couldn't sleep and stand, deep in meditation, until you notice your complete stillness and detached manner are making the guard feel uncomfortable, so you nod goodnight and return into the house. Turn to **77**.

64

As you reach out towards the slobbering man he balls his fist and drives it into your face, knocking you backwards. Lose 4 Endurance. If you are still alive, you spring to your feet and prepare to give battle. Turn to **56**.

65

You leap into the heaving, black, lava-like morass and lunge for the body of the goblin. A wave of intense pain burning like fire hits you; the digestive juices of the nameless horror strip the flesh of your legs from the bone as you force yourself to wade through its very being. Lose 9 Endurance. If you are still alive you haul yourself up the plaited vine and set it to swing gently, untying the goblin's body so that you can pull the bottom of the vine up out of the reach of the Primordial One. As the vine swings in an ever-greater arc, you catch sight of a flight of stone steps leading upwards beyond the goblins' god. Letting go, you somersault through the air and drop near the bottom step. As you look back, the horror is feeding on the remains of the goblin whose head is just disappearing below the heaving surface. Turn to 3.

66

You tell Kiyamo of the village and its problems. Immediately he orders Onikaba to send a detachment of Samurai to deal with it and you relax; the villagers will be safe. He speaks: 'Your fame has come before you, Ninja and Avenger. The followers of Vile, Nemesis and Vasch-Ro are howling for your blood whilst the followers of other gods are laughing up their sleeves. All that is clean and wholesome on Orb is rejoicing. I congratulate you,' and he bows before you. You thank him and he continues, 'But all is not well here, on the Island of Plenty. An evil daimio, Jikkyu, helped by his lieutenant, the master archer, Akira, has grown in power. He has gathered many Ronin and bandits to his banner. He also has an army of Bakemono or orcs marching with him. These he has won over with the help of unholy allies. My spies report that emissaries from the priests of Nemesis and the monks of Vile have promised Jikkyu much aid if, after he has conquered the Island of Plenty, he invades the Island of Tranquil Dreams and destroys it utterly. With the support of the priests of Nemesis, the monks of Vile and enough men, he could do it. Already he has subdued much of the south and he is massing his forces even now, just beyond the fortress of Kanokura. I, my men, and the blessings of the god, Eo, the Prince of Peace and Weal, are all that stand in his path. We were told of your coming, Ninja. We need your help. You must penetrate the enemy camp and slay Jikkyu. There is no other that can hold his alliance together. Not only is this to help us but also to protect your homeland. Leave the Scrolls of Kettsuin with us; the Grandmaster of the Dawn has sent a monk, Gorobei, to take them back should you fail in this mission, so that they cannot fall into enemy hands again. The Grandmaster said you would know him.'

He nods to his retainers who usher in the monk. You recognise the tall, powerful frame of Gorobei from the Temple of the Rock. He greets you and you embrace each other. 'It is good to see you again, Avenger,' he says, his eyes glistening with unshed tears. 'Long have we prayed for you.'

You decide to set off on your quest on the morrow. You hand the Scrolls of Kettsuin over to Gorobei. You are treated by the daimio's healers and you sleep well. You may restore up to 5 Endurance. The next day, Kiyamo shows you the whereabouts of Jikkyu's camp and you don your Ninja costume and set off. Turn to **48**.

67

If you are a skilled Lock-pick, turn to **184**. If not, read on. As your torch lights the dead-end of the spiralling tunnel a grinding noise makes you whirl round and you sprint back up the tunnel as a metal grille slides down from the ceiling, threatening to trap you, its bottom edge a series of rusty barbs. If you are a skilled Climber you may, if you wish, throw your grappling hook underneath it, hoping to wedge it above the floor (turn to **54**) or you may try to slide underneath it as if you were attempting the Dragon's Tail throw (turn to **39**).

68

As you swim towards the Dead Men's Fingers coral, three beings like manta rays with the heads of sharks swim towards you. They are intelligent and evil, the jackals of the sea. You decide to arm yourself with a piece of poisonous coral, clutching it in your fist so that the poisonous spikes protrude between your fingers. The Sea-Jackals swim to the attack. Turn to **111**.

69

Instead of a pass onto a trading ship, Hardred produces a throwing dagger which is flying to your heart before you can even recognise it for what it is. He throws too quickly for it to be Hardred. If you have the skill of Arrow Cutting turn to **342**. If you do not, this is the last thought you have as the dagger pierces your heart. The blade is grooved and covered in venom, but the steel alone has done its work. As you die 'Hardred' bows and says 'Mandrake, Guildmaster of Assassins, at your service, Ninja. Honoric will be pleased – for he still lives,

Ninja, in spite of your efforts.' You have failed.

70

The soldier hardly has time to realise what is happening to him as you slide down the stairs feet first; his sword jabs thin air. You twist your legs around his and then try to surge upwards and knock him down the staircase with your forearm.

KEEP GUARD
Defence against Dragon's Tail Throw: 5
Endurance: 12
Damage: 1 die

If you succeed turn to **130**. If you fail to knock him backwards as he crouches above you, he grips the hilt of his sword and, raising it above his head point downward, drives it at your abdomen in an attempt to skewer you. Your Defence is 6 as you try to roll aside and regain your footing on the stairs. If you are still alive after this, turn to **143**.

71

You steal into the cavern as the O-Bakemono rises to its feet. Stepping from the shadows you spit vigorously, and the needle hits the back of its neck. It clasps a hand over the wound and spins, roaring in pain. The young girl screams, wild hope in her eyes, and the Hannya twists to face you, a snarl of rage on her face. The O-Bakemono staggers but then swings its great club at you; it is still alive but weakened by the poison. You dodge the clumsy blow easily but several pulses of green energy fly from the fingers of the Hannya, exploding into your side and burning you. Lose 3 Endurance. If you are still alive, will you throw some Flash Powder into the fire (if you have any) and drive a Winged Horse kick at the O-Bakemono's temple (turn to **112**), spit another needle at it (turn to **139**), or hurl a Shuriken at the Hannya, whilst you try to finish off the O-Bakemono (turn to **152**)?

72

The goblins have not dared to cross the morass of ooze but, as you lope steadily on, their muffled cries tell you that they are approaching you but in a different tunnel. The one which you are running along is now lit with crude ornamental lanterns. You run onward until, rounding a corner, you surprise the biggest goblin you have ever seen. He has been counting out gold coins which he shoves under a cloth before picking up a long sword which is clearly not of goblin origin and which seems absurdly large for him to wield. He wears a dented copper crown and rusty ring-mail armour. You have still found no way out of the goblin caves but there is another tunnel behind the Goblin King. If you are skilled with Poison Needles you may wish to use one (turn to **339**), or you may hurl a Shuriken if you have one left (turn to **355**), or you may simply run to the attack (turn to **368**).

73

As you crouch and send a throwing star whistling through the air towards the leader, a pall of fear clouds your thoughts, but you triumph over it. Make a Shuriken Roll. If you score 8 or more, your throwing star beats the leader's shield and you may roll normally for the damage done to him. If you score 7 or less, the Shuriken embeds itself in his shield and he is unharmed as you move to attack. Will you use the Tiger's Paw chop (turn to **140**), the Leaping Tiger kick (turn to **154**) or the Whirlpool throw (turn to **163**)?

74

The face of the undead Barbarian is slack but the eyes within it are windows to a soul forfeited for-ever. You leap and drive the ball of your foot to-wards the dark eyes.

UNDEAD WARLORD
Defence against Leaping Tiger kick: 6
Endurance: 14
Damage: 1 Die + 2

If you have struck the undead Warlord for the first time turn to **30**. If the Warlord is dead turn to **37**. If it is still moving, it tries to cut your leg from your body in a heavy upward swipe of the chill gleaming sword. Your Defence as you try to hop aside is 8. If it hits you, you must subtract 2 from your next two die rolls as a numbing cold slows your reactions. If you are still alive, you may punch (turn to **86**), throw (turn to **53**) or kick again (return to the top of this paragraph).

75

The torturer grunts as your foot distorts his skull and he falls pole-axed to the floor. The young boy points and says, 'In the water, a way out,' just before the guards rush into the torture chamber. You decide to follow his advice and dive into the chill, dark depths of the pool knowing that if there is a way out to be found the heavily armoured guards will not be able to follow easily. At last you locate an underwater tunnel ahead of you. Make a Fate Roll but only roll one die. If you score a 1, 2, 3 or 4, turn to **80**. If you score a 5 or a 6, turn to **332**.

76

The tunnel twists and turns, ever deeper into the mountain. You are beginning to lose your sense of direction in the confusing darkness, but your torch burns brightly as you lope onward, breathing deeply, but as silently as a mouse. Turn to **113**.

77

You move from the light of the moon to the blackness of the interior and to the door that leads to the courtyard. You pull at the handle to slide it open, but it only moves a fraction before jamming – you try again but it won't move. In an instant all of your senses are alive and the hairs on your neck prickle with anticipation and suspicion. You crouch and turn quietly, convinced something is wrong. Then a sound reaches you from outside – a quiet but sharp sound, suddenly cut off, as if something metal had been dropped and then muffled before it could begin ringing. Will you go outside and investigate the noise (turn to **129**), hide behind one of the chests in the corner of the room (turn to **116**) or, if you have the skill of Lock-Picking, try to open the jammed door (turn to **148**)?

78

The hot liquid which pours into your belly is poison

but you are inured to it and you saw your teeth on the gristly stalk until the horrible bag-like thing jumps off you and scurries behind the rock. If you have killed the shaven-headed man, turn to **222**. If not, as you are recovering, the shaven-headed man's foot smashes into your skull in a version of the flying Winged Horse kick and you cartwheel away across the grass. Lose 7 Endurance. If you are still alive you roll to your feet and prepare to give battle. Turn to **56**.

79

From the edge of the torchlight you hurl a Shuriken and it embeds itself in the throat of one guard and he slumps with a slight gurgle. The other stares in horror as you are upon him, your Garotte around his neck. Just as he dies silently, there is a ripping sound and a long arrow shoots from inside the tent and into your side, its viciously barbed head bursting out at the other side, just below your ribs. You are spitted and slowly sink to your knees, strength fading, as a tall man with a curiously shaped longbow steps from the tent, smiling without humour. At least the Scrolls are safe . . . for now.

80

The tunnel down which you swim seems quite wide; you cannot feel the sides but swim strongly on. After a minute your head is still brushing the ceiling underwater but at last you emerge in a dank cavern, lit by a single, smoking torch. As the water runs from your costume you see the vague outline of what looks like one of the Elder gods, creatures that stalked the earth before man came from the stars. A great horn protrudes from its head and it stoops, almost brushing the tip against the fifteen foot-high ceiling. Its outline is strangely jagged and the smell of putrefaction suggests that its thick hide is sloughing off in great dead patches. If it is truly one of the Elder gods you know that it will be immensely strong even if weakened by its existence in this dank pit of slime. You see a half-eaten corpse, that of the unfortunate who was fed to the beast as you arrived at Quench-heart Keep. Its face is a mask of horror. Knowing that to return to the Keep itself would mean death you step forward, ready to give battle. Turn to **373**.

81

As you swim above the rippling, feathery, coral polyps three beings like manta rays with the heads of sharks swim towards you. They are intelligent and evil, the jackals of the deep, and they swim to attack you. Turn to **111**.

82

You protest your innocence but Tyutchev merely says, 'Then we will kill you anyway, just for the joy of sword-play.' He and Cassandra advance upon you from either side while Thaum begins to mutter a spell. Will you attack Cassandra (turn to **121**), call upon Kwon the Redeemer to help you, if you have not done so already (turn to **59**), use an item you may have picked up on your travels (turn to **147**), or if you are skilled with Poison Needles you may wish to use one (turn to **170**)?

83

You spin and leap, punching and kicking, but they are reckless and one sacrifices himself, hurling himself at you bodily. You kill him with a single blow but his body weighs you down and the others overpower you through sheer weight of numbers. They have regained the Scrolls of Kettsuin and you are thrown into the harbour and left to drown amid the tangled nets of the fishermen.

84

The voyage passes uneventfully. The *Winged Serpent* gives the port city of Doomover a wide berth and at last sails up the River Greybones to Tor, the city that invented Torean fire, balls of exploding flames used in battles at sea.

You are overjoyed to see Glaivas, the Ranger Lord whose news started you on your long journey, on the wharf and you welcome him aboard. The master lends the pair of you his cabin and goes in search of his favourite dive. Glaivas' look of admiration as you tell him of your exploits almost embarrasses you but he turns at last to matters of the moment. He has not been idle; he is now general of the Torean army, ready to march against the Legion of the Sword of Doom at any time. He bids you farewell late that night and the ship sets sail for Lemné, on the Island of Plenty, in the morning. You wonder if you will ever see him again, but are thankful to have by-passed the perils of the Manmarch. You still have four hundred leagues of ocean to cross but you feel at one with the world. Several days later, you anchor in the bustling harbour of Lemné with its fishing boats and junks. Turn to **11**.

85

Your fist explodes towards the face of the soldier like a battering-ram as you bend your knees to strike under his guard. He tries to bring down the lower rim of his shield against your forearm.

KEEP GUARD
Defence against Iron Fist punch: 6
Endurance: 12
Damage: 1 die

If you succeed, the force of your punch rocks him but he comes on again, thrusting with his sword. Turn to **219**. If you missed him the rim of his shield cracks against the Iron Sleeves of your forearm and you are unhurt, much to the Keep guard's surprise. Next he slashes at you with his long sword, trying to cut your legs from under you. Your Defence is 8 as you try to leap high above the whistling blade. After this blow, you may use the Tiger's Paw chop (turn to **233**) or the Winged Horse kick (turn to **101**).

86

The undead Barbarian Warlord lumbers towards you, its dark eyes pits of evil. You decide to put all of your strength into your blow, using the Iron Fist punch.

UNDEAD WARLORD
Defence against Iron Fist punch: 5
Endurance: 14
Damage: 1 Die + 2

If you have struck the undead Warlord for the first time turn to **30**. If the Warlord is beaten, turn to **37**. If it is still moving, it tries to claw you and strike you with its glowing sword. You try to parry its lumbering blows with your sleeve-guards, and your Defence is 9. If it hits you, you must subtract 2 from

your next two dice rolls as a numbing cold slows your reactions. If you are still alive, you may kick (turn to **74**), throw (turn to **53**) or punch again (return to the top of this paragraph).

87

He thrusts at your chest. You act quickly, stepping in and blocking his sword-arm with your left arm and then twisting with him, trying to yank him over your hip and to the ground.

NINJA
Defence against Whirlpool throw: 6
Endurance: 19
Damage: 1 Die + 2

If you are successful, you throw him over your hip but he flips in mid-air and lands agilely on his feet, spinning to face you. However, your next attack catches him unprepared. You may either use the Tiger's Paw chop (turn to **304**) or the Forked Lightning Strike kick (turn to **55**), adding 1 to your Attack Modifier for this attack only. If you have failed to throw the Ninja, turn to **133**.

88

The pale, lidless eyes swim from the flame, but the black mass of its amorphous body merely ripples away from it, almost unharmed. You drive the torch at the nearest tongue of jelly but the Primordial One flows around you until you are inside a hollow circle

with the heaving monster all around you. As the torch begins to die, you realise that you will have to try and run through it to the dangling vine. Turn to **65**.

89

You pull the Dancing Sword from where it is strapped to your back and point it at Tyutchev, waving it in the air before taking your hands away in the hope that it will attack him on its own. Unfortunately, you do not know how to trigger its magic and it falls to the floor. You parry Tyutchev's blow but Cassandra's sword bites coldly into your back and your lungs fill with blood. You die, coughing blood, and they will use the knowledge contained in the Scrolls of Kettsuin to wreak havoc on Orb. You have failed.

90

The tunnel bends in an ever-sharper spiral, deep into the cold, grey bones of the rock. You can tell that no-one has passed this way for a long time and still there is no movement in the air. Will you go to find what lies at the end of the spiral (turn to **67**) or retrace your steps and go on down the main tunnel (turn to **76**)?

91

You jog onward, following the road, towards the palace of the daimio, Kiyamo. The countryside is green and lush, with many valleys. Paddy-fields fill most of the valleys for the Island of Plenty is extensively farmed.

There is much activity on the roads; wagons laden with supplies and troops of warriors, footmen,

Samurai and cavalry pass you often. They are all soldiers of Kiyamo and wear red lacquered armour laced together with white ribbons. Their banners, strapped to the backs of the bannermen or Hatemoto, depict a four pointed star within a quatrefoil, red on white, the symbol or Mons of Lord Kiyamo. It seems war is at hand. After a time the road forks – the right leads onto the mountain pass and the fortress of Kanokura, an important strongpoint. You take the less travelled route to the left, leading to the Palace of Kiyamo in the mountains. You travel on alone for a while until you see the smoke of a village some way to the right, surrounded by paddy-fields, set before the foothills of the mountains. You jog towards the village and into the main square, surrounded by the few wooden houses that make up the village. You hope for food – it is the early afternoon and you have been jogging continuously for some hours. But nobody is about. You pause in the village, looking around you. Your keen sense of hearing picks up a heavy sobbing, as of someone in terrible grief, from a nearby house. Opening the door you see a small weather-beaten man, his back bent by years of toil in the fields, comforting his wife, a rather large woman, red-faced and crying hopelessly. You ask what is happening. The man looks up in surprise, his face wracked with grief. A look of hope sparks in his eyes as he looks you up and down. 'Help us, sir,' he says. 'An evil Hannya and her servant, an O-Bakemono have come to live in a cave nearby and have been leeching us of our food and what little money we have.'

'Why have you not resisted,' you ask, 'or asked for help from the palace soldiery?'

'The O-Bakemono killed four of our young men at

once, sir, and their cave is near the road. The Hannya has sorcerous powers, sir, and seems able to detect anyone who passes along the road – no-one dares to tell the palace; nor has anyone passed through or dallied here for any length of time, save you sir – the times are troubled, what with war in the south, and now . . .' He almost breaks down into tears at this point. 'The Hannya has taken our daughter to be sacrificed in two days' time to the evil demon she worships – Baal, Lord of the Flies. Help us, noble lord, help us!'

You decide you must help them – will you go to the cave and try to kill the beings and release the girl (turn to **402**), or press on as fast as you can to the palace where you are needed and send a large detachment of soldiers back to do the job; they can be here within a day (turn to **36**)?

92

As you wash the grey slime off your costume your hand touches a piece of cold metal in the shallow pool. Your fingers curl around a small box stuck in a crack which you prise out and then open. It contains what appears to be no more than a brass signet ring.

You put it on and replace the box in the pool before continuing on your way once more. Make a note of the brass signet ring on your Character Sheet. Turn to 72.

93

Tearing your eyes away from the vision in the opal ring, you leap over the heads of the nearest onlookers and quit the Great Hall before the slow barbarians can move. Ulrik's Haven is soon far behind you as you travel south and then west across the wild terrain towards Wargrave Abbas. Turn to 131.

94

The small Poison Needle which you spit at the brigand leader pierces his neck and he convulses horribly and is soon dead. The other brigands, who saw nothing and believe you must have the power to cast death spells, break and run. You walk up to the fallen man to look his body over. Turn to 297.

95

You are suddenly at the centre of a brilliant globe of silver light. Kwon has answered your prayer and you float into another plane, passing through the rock walls as if they were no more substantial than webs of gossamer. Your god does not talk to you and you are conscious of a feeling of ancient and powerful malevolence. Your hopes are dashed when you feel that the glowing light is forced away from you by some ancient evil, and you are still below ground, instead of beneath the calm, blue sky. As you walk along in the ghostly light which seems to come from the rocks themselves, a feeling of grim foreboding wells up within you. Kwon has saved you from death but you know that you will be called upon soon to repay your debt. You may not ask Kwon for Salvation again until you reach the Island of Tranquil Dreams. Turning a corner, your torch half lights a repellent and terrifying sight. Turn to **174**.

96

You jump and grab a supporting wooden strut and swing up onto the tiled roof as agilely and as silently as a cat. You crawl along the roof until you can see over and down to the steps in front of the house. At the foot of the steps lies the Samurai guard, face down. A ribbon of blood, almost black in the dull light, oozes from his neck into the earth. What is unmistakably a Shuriken, almost identical to your own, is embedded in the back of his neck. It is silver, seeming to glow in the moonlight, and inlaid with thin bands of ebony shaped into a whirlpool or vortex symbol. Will you drop quietly down to the main doors at the front of the house (turn to **10**) or stay where you are and await events (turn to **123**)?

97

You swim powerfully to the surface, as dark shadows like flying beasts pass beneath you. Above you a merman's blood stains the sea, like a brown

streamer in the wind. A whale with a six foot slender horn on its forehead is swimming straight towards him and he twists and turns, feebly avoiding its savage thrust. Will you ignore the merman and, avoiding the whale, swim on to the surface (turn to **160**) or swim to his aid (turn to **136**)?

98

Without a sound you work your way to the back of the tent and, using Cassandra's dagger, tear a small hole in the canvas and look through. Inside, it is large and spacious lit by several lanterns and littered with the paraphernalia of a commander on the march. Two men are poring over a large map on a table. One is big and bulky, arrogantly handsome, the other tall and lean, a curiously shaped longbow slung on his back. The handsome man says, in a rich mellow voice, 'No, Akira, it must be the pass.' The other replies, 'But surely, my lord Jikkyu, Kiyamo will be expecting that.' And so the discussion goes on.

Will you widen the hole and hurl a Shuriken at Jikkyu (turn to **126**), place a Poisoned Needle in your bamboo breathing-tube and blow it at Jikkyu if you have that skill (turn to **114**) or wait for a better opportunity – perhaps Akira will leave the room (turn to **145**)?

99

Nothing happens. Kwon cannot hear you, deep in the caverns, in the presence of the Primordial One, for the goblins worship it and it is truly a god to them. The seething black mass of lava-like jelly flows around you and its digestive juices start to dissolve your skin. Lose 5 Endurance. If you are still alive, the pain temporarily releases you from its hold. Will you drive your fist into the amorphous mass (turn to **117**), use a Poison Needle if you have the skill (turn to **102**) or use your torch on it (turn to **88**)?

100

Your training has made it possible to struggle against the horror in the moat for several minutes but you no longer have the strength to hurt it. It drags you down into the slime at the bottom and as you drown the events of your life flash before you. You try to call out to Kwon but your lungs fill with water and you die in the murk of the moat which surrounds Quench-heart Keep.

101

Your foot lashes out at the guard's head as he flails his sword through the air. It is easier for you to strike home when kicking from a higher position as you are now.

KEEP GUARD
Defence against Winged Horse kick: 5
Endurance: 12
Damage: 1 die

If you have killed the Keep guard, turn to **249**. Otherwise, you must try to leap above the blade of his long sword as he tries to cut at your leg. Your Defence, as you leap up on one foot after kicking, is 7. If you are still alive, you may use the Tiger's Paw chop (turn to **233**) or kick again (return to the top of this paragraph).

102

Your skill with Poison Needles allows you to blow one into the nearest pale and lidless eye. The nameless horror contracts and you have a moment in which to act freely. Will you risk a great leap to swing on the plaited vine which dangles the body of a goblin above the seething horror (turn to **62**), or use your torch on it (turn to **88**)?

103

Desperately you claw at the Garotte but soon your body has no oxygen to power its muscles and your legs give way beneath you. Your arms fall lifeless at your sides; you struggle to lift them but they are like lead and your lungs burn with fire. The wire cuts into the flesh of your neck but you can no longer feel it as, mercifully, you fall into a black nothingness.

104

As you walk along in the ghostly light, which comes from the rocks all around you, a feeling of grim foreboding wells up within you. Turning a corner your torch half lights a repellent and terrifying sight. Turn to **174**.

105

The adviser's brow is furrowed with effort; his eyes dart from left to right. 'Where are you, stranger?' you hear him say. 'Why can I not see you? You must be the one, the killer of Manse the Deathmage.' At length the sight of his face fades and the opal is opaque once more. Realising that the adviser reveres Nemesis, you leap above the nearest rank of onlookers and rush to the door. But you never make it. The adviser is there before you and he casts a spell which locks it shut. The barbarians give voice to awful battle cries – you are surrounded and cannot break out. They beat down your defences at last and you are killed. The Scrolls of Kettsuin are pilfered by the adviser who will flee the city on the morrow. The Scrolls have fallen into the possession of those who worship Nemesis, the Supreme Principle of Evil. You have failed.

106

Inexplicably, a chill of fear runs through you as they draw their swords. If they are mere brigands they should pose little threat. As you approach in fighting stance you notice that they stand together, awaiting your attack like trained soldiers, not bandits. Which type of move will you choose as you unleash the power of your body: a Leaping Tiger kick (turn to **154**), Tiger's Paw chop (turn to **140**), or a Whirlpool throw (turn to **163**)?

107

You call upon Kwon the Redeemer to be your salvation but he will not come to your aid again so soon. The torturer takes the axe from his belt with great deliberation, an evil smile spreading across his lips beneath the black leather hood. The guards burst into the chamber behind you and you have no time to kill him before they are upon your back. Will you plunge into the pool and swim to the back wall (turn to **153**) or surrender to the torturer (turn to **124**)?

108

Tyutchev and Cassandra are advancing upon you from either side, while Thaum begins to mutter a spell. Which one of them will you send your throwing star towards: Cassandra (turn to **209**), Tyutchev (turn to **187**) or Thaum (turn to **198**)?

109

You sink gradually into the clammy ooze and are almost thankful when the goblins appear behind you in the tunnel for you will surely sink below the surface within seconds. When the goblins begin to pelt you with stones there is nothing you can do; if you raise your arms you will sink straightaway. You decide to call upon your god, Kwon the Redeemer, to save you. If you have not yet called upon him, turn to **95**. If you have already called on him, your prayers are unanswered and the clammy slime sucks your bruised head below the surface, filling your lungs with slime. At least the Scrolls of Kettsuin will rot with you.

110

After two long minutes, during which Ulrik Skarsang's eyes never leave yours, the adviser returns and looking at you beneath veiled lids, pronounces that it is safe to let you stay in Ulrik's Haven. You ask about ships sailing to the far south and Ulrik tells you that the only ship sailing to the far south is his personal merchantman, the *Sack of the South*, but that she will not return to port for two tendays. He says that you are welcome to free passage and offers to settle you in the house of a farmer until the ship is ready to sail. You accept his offer and walk a little way off to think things over. If you decide that twenty days is too long to wait and journey instead towards Wargrave Abbas, turn to **179**. If you decide to rest in Ulrik's Haven before taking ship, turn to **33**.

111

The Sea-Jackals circle around you, then dart in for

the kill, their great wings making them look like prehistoric birds of the sea. If you are not carrying some Dead Men's Fingers coral in your fist you may try a Cobra Strike (turn to **245**). If you are, you try to use the Iron Fist punch to bury the coral spikes into a Sea-Jackal's snout. His Defence as you try to do this is 5. If you fail, the coral is knocked from your grasp and you may try another Cobra Strike (turn to **245**), or, alternatively, if you are skilled with Poison Needles you may prefer to use these (turn to **279**). If you succeed with the coral turn to **292**.

112

You throw the powder onto the fire and close your eyes. There is a blinding flash, filling the cavern with the light of day. Looking up, you see the O-Bakemono has dropped its club; its hands are over its eyes, moaning, whilst the Hannya is shaking her head and shrieking in frustration, trying to clear her vision. You sidestep the O-Bakemono and, taking your time, unleash a perfect Winged Horse at its temple, letting out a cry as you do so. There is a crack and it goes down like a stone. You turn to face the Hannya as her vision clears to focus upon you. Turn to **390**.

113

The tunnel curves round in an 'S' bend and then your way is barred by a heavy gate. Warily you push the gate open and slip through into a dimly lit cavern. Holes in the roof allow beams of daylight into the cavern which is covered by what looks like a moving black carpet. High-pitched chirruping sounds all around you and as you walk across the cavern a pain in your leg, as you are bitten, tells you that the moving carpet is in fact a sea of black rats. Grain has been strewn underfoot and they are

preoccupied with eating. You run across the cavern, heedless of the rats underfoot and there is a clamour behind you. A party of goblins with short, stabbing swords are chasing you. You leave the passage, pass a grain store, and realise that the goblins are farming the rats for meat. Revolted, you run along a tunnel which leads ever-deeper into the mountain. Turn to **127**.

114

As quietly as possible, you insert the bamboo tube into the hole unnoticed and spit a needle at Jikkyu's throat. You are on target, but somehow, incredibly, it has little effect, leaving only a slight gash to mark its passage – he is unaffected by the poison. As you stare, momentarily astonished, Akira lets fly an arrow aimed just above the hole you have made. It slams into your left eye and on into your brain, killing you instantly.

115

As the nameless horror threatens to engulf you, you mouth the words of the Covenant. When you reach the phrase, 'I will be killed many times, yet will not die,' you are able to draw on the mental powers of your training as a Ninja, and you can move again. Will you use your torch on the amorphous mass (turn to **88**), use a Poison Needle if you have the skill (turn to **102**), or risk a great leap to swing on the plaited vine that dangles the body of a goblin above it (turn to **62**)?

116

You glide to the corner of the room and crouch silently behind a large chest, unmoving, your breathing shallow and soundless. A few moments pass – sweat trickles from your brow, the nape of your neck crawls and every sense is straining. Then there is a faint sound, almost indetectable. You are not sure whether it came from outside or from within the room. Will you stay where you are (turn to 165) or move around the edge of the room to the main doors and, opening them slightly, step out (turn to 137)?

117

Your fist sinks in deep, but the flesh of your arm is stripped away by contact with the black jelly-like morass. A great wave takes shape inside the name-less horror and it washes over you, engulfing you in its ingesting embrace. As the black amorphous jelly flows around you and its juices eat at your skin, your heart fails you. At least the Scrolls of Kettsuin will be digested with you!

118

The opal ring on your finger glows suddenly and Ulrik notices this. As you look down at it the gem-stone seems to glow until it fills your field of vision. It clears as if a mist had been blown out of it and the hatchet-face of Ulrik Skarsang's adviser appears, a black whirlpool now painted on his right cheek. If you choose this moment to attempt to flee Ulrik's Haven, turn to 93 and read no further. If you hesitate, turn to 105.

119

One of the goblins jabs his sword into your leg, as you toss another over your shoulder and down the precipice. You catch his arm, but a third head-butts you in the groin and you lose your balance and fall a hundred feet. Your torch is lost and you are in darkness. Fate has not deserted you entirely, however, for you land on top of your victim, crushing the last glimmer of life out of him as he softens your landing, but you have lost 8 Endurance. If you are still alive, you pick yourself up, light another torch and walk along a narrow shelf lit by a faint phosphorescence where a small tunnel meets the chasm into which you have fallen. Turn to **104**.

120

With the agility of a spider-monkey, you launch yourself at the branch and swing up amongst the leaves of the tree just as an envenomed dagger hurtles beneath you. The man posing as Hardred gapes for a moment, then turns to run. You drop down from the tree and follow but the gardener with whom you exchanged pleasantries this morning emerges from behind the magnolia tree, blocking your way. On the steps of the temple the real Hardred beckons urgently. You run to him but he says, 'Gently, but yes, good news; a ship sails for Tor on the evening tide. I can vouch for the master.' You look around but the imposter has fled and the gardener is nowhere to be seen. Turn to **289**.

121

You move quickly away from Tyutchev and Thaum and towards Cassandra. She crouches, waiting like a cat for you to move, her sword glowing coldly with evil magic. Will you try the Dragon's Tail throw (turn to **232**), the Forked Lightning strike kick (turn to **248**) or the Iron Fist punch (turn to **254**)?

122

Your foot strikes a submerged boulder and you are able to thrust yourself towards the edge of the clammy ooze and are then lucky enough to grab onto firm ground once more. You pull yourself out and continue on your way, towards a large cavern. Before you reach it you see a pool at the side of the tunnel. Will you hurry past it (turn to **72**) or use it to wash the grey filth from your garments (turn to **92**)?

123

You wait for some minutes, your senses straining. Nothing. Then you can feel a tingling in between your shoulder blades, as if someone's eyes were burning into you. You leap up and whirl around, and gasp in surprise. There is a figure, dressed as you, save for a curved scabbarded sword or Ninjato strapped to his back, creeping stealthily towards you, black eyes glinting malevolently in the moonlight. He stops dead and snarls as you spot him, but in the second of your surprise his hand flickers in and out and a Shuriken almost identical to your own, buries itself in your shoulder. Lose 3 Endurance. If you are still alive, the force of the blow sends you off balance and you topple over the edge of the roof. Are you skilled at Acrobatics? If you are, turn to **182**. If you are not, turn to **159**.

124

You bow to the torturer and hold out your hands. His lips part in an evil grin beneath his black, leather hood as he binds you with ropes. The soldiers clatter into the chamber and inform him that you have killed Yaemon, Honoric and Manse the Death-mage. The torturer's voice fills with false anger. 'I can see my ingenuity will be stretched to the limit thinking up fitting punishments for you, Ninja.' He tells the soldiers to prepare a set of heated manacles in the furnace and goes off to fetch some of his 'special devices'.

Are you a skilled Escapologist? If you are not, turn to **344**. If you are, the torturer returns a moment later with an iron helmet which opens in half but has two spikes on the inside where the wearer's eyes would be. The spikes can be screwed gradually inward, a turn at a time. He orders the guards from the chamber and turns to examine the manacles in a small furnace. Using your skill as an Escapologist you dislocate one arm and by tensing certain muscles and inching your steel-like fingers between the bonds, you struggle free. Mercifully, the boy remains silent as you creep like a stalking tiger towards the broad, sweating back of the torturer. With a cry you explode into a kick which sends his head flying into the furnace. The boy cheers weakly as you close the furnace door on the neck of the sadistic torturer, muffling his death agonies. You free the prisoners and the boy tells you that there is a way of escape through the underground river which connects the pool in this chamber to the moat. Knowing that you must restore the Scrolls of Kettsuin to safety, you thank him and dive in. Turn to **153**.

125

You launch your feet at his legs in a move calculated to take him by surprise but his reactions are not those of an imbecile. His Defence against your Dragon's Tail throw is 7 as he tries to leap above your scything legs. If you throw him successfully you are in a perfect position to use the Forked Lightning strike as he rises to his feet; turn to **169**. If you fail, he stamps downward on your leg – subtract one from your Kick Modifier as your thigh muscles bleed internally, and lose 4 Endurance. If you are still alive, you roll aside and spring to the attack again. Will you throw (return to top of this paragraph), punch (turn to **142**) or kick (turn to **169**)?

126

Suddenly you rip the canvas open and jump into the tent, to be greeted by gasps of astonishment. With blurring speed you hurl a Shuriken at Jikkyu's throat. Your throw is accurate but somehow, incredibly, it has little effect, leaving only a slight gash to mark its passage. In a moment Akira has an arrow ready in his bow and Jikkyu has shouted for the guards. You manage to avoid Akira's first arrow but soon the guards are upon you and, whilst you despatch them with a series of kicks and punches, Akira has sent another arrow straight through your neck and out the other side. It is all over and you die in a pool of blood.

127

As you run on, the tumult behind you increases. Although you have not seen a turning or side tunnel, more goblins seem to have joined in the chase. Rounding yet another corner you are faced with a fork in the passage. Will you take the left fork which shows signs of heavy wear (turn to **146**) or the right, which does not (turn to **162**)?

128

The magician makes as if to give you the gleaming

golden-jewelled ring but a yellow star bursts from it, exploding against your chest with the force of a ball of Torean fire. Lose 9 Endurance. If you are still alive, turn to **204**.

129

You pull the front door open again; the Samurai has gone! Cautiously, you step out and to the side. Still he is nowhere. You edge forward crab-like, legs apart, knees bent, arms straight out and down to either side in a defensive stance of the Way of the Tiger. You come to the edge of the pillared cloister of the boardwalk at the front of the house and to the top of the steps that lead down to the stone path, lit by the two lanterns. There! At the foot of the steps lies the Samurai guard, face down. A ribbon of blood, almost black in the dull light, oozes from his neck into the earth. What is unmistakably a Shuriken, almost identical to your own, is embedded in the back of his neck. It is silver, seeming to glow in the moonlight and inlaid with thin bands of ebony shaped into a whirlpool or vortex symbol.

Suddenly you hear a rush of air behind you and you start to turn but there is a sharp pain around your throat and something slams into your back. You are pulled backwards, and dragged into the house as the Garotte, for that is what it is, you realise with a sickened sense of familiarity, tightens horribly, choking the life from you. You desperately try to reach or kick behind you, or leap high and somer-sault over your assailant, but he seems to realise what you are able to do, for he drags you back-wards, continuously. You have no time to regain your balance. You struggle for breath and waves of blackness seem to engulf your vision. The folds of your hood prevent severe laceration from the thin wire, but it is beginning to bite. Through a haze of swirling colour and rushing noise as death comes nearer, you hear a hissed whisper in your ear. 'I am Ninja. I follow the Way of the Scorpion. I give your soul to Nemesis.' Do you have the ability to Feign Death? If you do, turn to **189**. If you do not, turn to **103**.

130

The Keep guard is thrown off his feet by the power of your upward surge and the soldier into whose arms he has fallen cannot hold him. They both fall backwards down the staircase, causing chaos amongst the rest of the soldiers who are trying to reach you. After much cursing and struggling they reorganise themselves, and a great mountain of a man, the Bailiff's bodyguard, strides powerfully up the stairs to do battle with you. You may sprint across the roof of the Keep and try an enormous leap, hoping to clear the castle wall and land in the moat far below (turn to **34**) or stay to do battle (turn to **161**).

131

The road to Wargrave Abbas is a long, hard one. You pass through the towns of Chaddy, Steeplefell and Cheaping Knowe, spending a restful night in each. You may restore any lost Endurance. The road now runs along the banks of the Crow river and you eagerly increase your pace; soon you see the fields that surround the city of Wargrave Abbas. The city itself is on an island in the delta of the river. Just north of the gates is a beautiful public garden. Curbing your impatience to see the sea you decide to sit on a low wooden bench to meditate. To your surprise, a monk bearing the celestial symbol of Kwon the Redeemer passes by. You follow him through a stand of Rhododendron bushes and a

cloistered monastery comes into sight. You step inside, shed your peasant's garb and bow deeply to the Grandmaster, Hardred. You pray in a temple filled with flowers and your spirit feels lighter – you regain one point of Inner Force.

Telling Hardred of your mission lifts a great weight off your mind. He says he has heard rumours and that he is honoured to have you with him. He tells you that you look a little haggard and suggests that you stay in the monastery while he arranges for passage on a ship sailing south. You accept gracefully, telling him that you would like to call at the port of Tor, to see the Ranger Lord Glaivas, who first told you of the whereabouts of Yaemon, Grandmaster of Flame, if that is possible. Hardred smiles and says that if it is possible it shall be accomplished. He even suggests that you leave the Scrolls of Kettsuin in his care but you decline, saying that their rightful place is in the Temple of the Rock. Your sleep that night is filled with pleasant dreams of your homeland. Turn to **408**.

132

Such is your training in the powers of mind over matter that you can actually force yourself to think as though the nameless horror which threatens to engulf you did not exist. But it does no good. The seething black mass of lava-like jelly flows around you and its digestive juices start to dissolve your skin. Lose 5 Endurance. If you are still alive, will you drive your fist into the amorphous mass (turn to **117**), use a Poison Needle if you have the skill (turn to **102**), or use your torch on it (turn to **88**)?

133

As you turn to the Ninja, his left arm snakes around

and you can see a ring in his hand, two spikes pointed inward at his palm. Before you can disengage, he has grabbed your wrist tightly, the needles puncturing your costume and your skin. He shouts in triumph, and you dive forward, somersault and come to your feet, turning to face him. If you do not have Immunity to Poisons turn to **256**. If you have this skill and this is the first time the Ninja has tried to poison you, turn to **263**. If you have previously used this skill to counter poison attempts by the Ninja, turn to **191**.

134

One of the goblins thrusts savagely with his sword, but you sidestep it and, grabbing his sword-arm, use a Whirlpool Throw to send him into the depths. The other goblin slashes your thigh as your back is momentarily turned. Lose 3 Endurance. If you are still alive, you despatch him with a Forked Lightning strike and then force your way through the others and run on down the tunnel, deeper into the mountain. Turn to **149**.

135

You pass through the town of Bourton Abbas and leave the lowlands of the Crow Valley behind. You sleep well in the uplands and you may restore any Endurance you have lost. After five days' travel, the port of Ulrik's Haven lies before you. The city is well defended against attack by sea but there is no guard on the land-gate, so you walk straight to the beach where a number of large galleys and smaller fishing boats are pulled up on the sand, or riding at anchor. When you ask for passage on a ship sailing south you have a little trouble understanding their uncouth barbarian dialect. But the gist of what they say is that no merchant would be fool enough to send a trading vessel to Ulrik's Haven where it would be seized and its crew put to death. As you strive to understand the captain of what is obviously a raiding ship, four burly men approach with swords drawn.

They demand gruffly that you go with them to meet their liege-chief. You decide to go along with them, hoping to find out more information from their leader. They seem satisfied that you will give no trouble and say nothing as you walk towards a long wooden building. Inside is a great hall with a large fire burning and a boar roasting above it on a spit. The hall is full of people and a grizzled old barbarian with a cunning gleam in his eye sits on a wooden throne, his advisers beside him. Your escorts nod their heads in what passes for a bow as they halt before him. Will you bow (turn to 329) or stare defiantly at the Barbarian Overlord (312)?

136

Seeing you, the merman summons the last shreds of his failing strength and darts behind you, as the Narwhal closes in once more. If you would like to try grabbing its horn and then kicking its large eye, turn to 208. If you would rather wait to see what it will do, turn to 223.

137

You stand and pause, but can see, hear or smell nothing unusual. Like a panther you steal around the walls of the room, head cautiously turning towards the door. Nothing happens, but it seems all your senses are shrieking a warning though everything is quiet, the air is still and only the faint chirruping of crickets intrudes into your consciousness. Turn to 129.

138

You have only a few seconds to beat the burly torturer before the guards surround you. If you have no Inner Force left, you kick out as he goes for his axe. Turn to **58**. If you have Inner Force you decide to use it and, leaping across the torture chamber, you unleash a flying Forked Lightning Strike of awesome power at his chest and head. Deduct 1 from your Inner Force. The torturer is too slow to defend against this kick but you will need to make a Kick Roll of 8 or more if you are to fell him with one attack. If you manage this, turn to **75**. If you fail, turn to **58**.

139

You spit another needle at the scaly beast and it staggers back, fatally poisoned, howling in pain. At the same time, another flurry of green bolts leaps from the Hannya's fingers into your side. Lose another 3 Endurance as you gasp and double over. If you are still alive, the O-Bakemono crashes into the large fire, and the flames soar upward, consuming it. You spin to face the Hannya. Turn to **390**.

140

You decide to concentrate your attacks against their

leader but if you do not fell him quickly you will be overwhelmed, for they fight with the skill of highly trained warriors, not mere brigands. Count how many times you try to kick, punch or throw him. You chop with lightning speed at the leader's unprotected neck as he drives his sword towards you.

BRIGAND LEADER
Defence against Tiger's Paw chop: 6
Endurance: 15
Damage: 1 Die + 2

If you win, turn to **297**. If he still lives you must defend against his thrust (your Defence is 7) and against the cut of one of his men (your Defence is 6). You may block only one. All of the brigands do the same damage as their leader when they hit. If you have attacked him four times and he still lives, turn to **337**. If not and if you still live, you may now kick (turn to **154**), throw (turn to **163**) or punch the leader again (return to the top of this paragraph).

141

As you glide down the tunnel which bends around some outjutting blocks of a hard red rock the cries of your pursuers ring hollowly behind you. As you round a red-painted boulder, your feet sink into a dark greyish ooze which is like quicksand. Make a Fate Roll. If Fate smiles on you, turn to **122**. If Fate turns her back on you turn to **109**.

142

Your fist lashes out at the shaven-headed man but he steps back and chops his hands onto your forearm and upper arm, breaking your elbow. You lose 5 Endurance and must subtract 1 from your Punch Modifier, as it will heal badly. If you are still alive, you notice a Scarlet Mantis tattooed on his forehead, but made faint with cornflour. You decide not to risk a punch again. Will you use the Dragon's Tail throw (turn to 125) or the Forked Lightning Strike kick (turn to 169)?

143

You struggle to your feet and spring backwards to the top of the staircase. The Keep guard lunges at you once more. You hop backwards again and he misses but he has gained the roof of the Keep and is quickly followed by several more soldiers. You will soon be surrounded. You may sprint across the roof of the Keep and try an enormous leap, hoping to clear the castle wall and land in the moat far below (turn to 34), take the first opportunity to use the skill of Feigning Death if you have it (turn to 178), throw some Flash Powder onto the glowing charcoal brazier if you have any left (turn to 192) or fight it out (turn to 206).

144

You sleep below a hawthorn tree but your dreams are troubled. Guilt seems to gather around you like a grey fog, crushing your spirit. You feel as if you had done wrong in killing the young magician and that no good will come of it. Subtract one from your Fate Modifier. You spend some time trying to activate the magic of the ring but realise that without a magical trigger word it is useless to you. You hurl it into the undergrowth, hoping that any curse it brings may leave you. Cross it off your Character Sheet. If you have been through the caves of the goblins, turn to **213**. If not, your sleep has at least restored your strength. You regain up to 2 points of lost Endurance. In the morning the birds trill loudly as you climb another hill to see if you can catch sight of the Endless Sea, but it is far beyond the horizon. Will you head south-west, a way which looks rough and woody (turn to **44**), or due west where the land is more open and there is less cover (turn to **32**)?

145

As you wait, your keen senses pick up something strange about Jikkyu. The outline of his head seems to blur and a hideous demonic visage is superimposed over it for a brief moment. Was it a trick of the poor light or is Jikkyu not what he appears to be, you ask yourself? Then Akira looks up straight at the hole you have made, his throat exposed, and his eyes widen in shock. You have only a moment in which to act. Will you hurl a Shuriken – if you have one – at Akira's throat (turn to **197**), leap into the tent and spit a needle at Akira's throat, if you have that skill (turn to **214**), leap in and hurl a Shuriken – again, if you have one – at Jikkyu (turn to **126**) or spit a needle at Jikkyu, if you have that skill (turn to **269**)?

146

As the hubbub behind you grows more distant the passageway widens out and you are suddenly faced with two goblins, larger than the rest, riding giant rats. They carry wooden spears with stone tips and as they charge they lower them like lances. If you are a skilled Acrobat turn to **190**. If you still have a Shuriken and would like to throw one in the instant before impact turn to **203**. Otherwise you try to knock their makeshift lances aside; turn to **228**.

147

It occurs to you to make use of one of the following, if you possess any of them:

A gleaming Sun-Star ring (turn to **47**).
A Dancing Sword (turn to **89**).
A Crystal gem containing water (turn to **8**).

Or if you do not possess or do not wish to use any of these, turn to **43** and choose again.

148

You reach into a pocket of your costume and draw out a long, flat strip of metal. You insert it between door and wall and move it up – it comes up against something and you give a little push. Whatever it is falls off the other side of the door with a quiet clatter and lands on the floor of the inner courtyard. Dropping to rest on your haunches, you slide the door open and spin through, your senses still screaming with a thrill of unseen danger. As you close the door you see a short length of metal with a hook at either end on the floor. Somebody must have deliberately jammed it shut from the courtyard. You turn to scan the inner courtyard and the edges of the roof when you hear a muffled sound from the room you have

just come from, a faint scraping – perhaps not a sound at all.

What will you do? You may wish to scale the wall of the inner courtyard to the roof, an easy climb for which you do not need the skill of Climbing (turn to **96**). You may press your back against the wall, melting in the shadows to the right of the door you have just come through (turn to **177**) or open the door and go back into the first room of the house as quickly and as quietly as possible (turn to **212**).

149

You can run faster than the bow-legged goblins, but they know the tunnels which are their home. You turn a sharp bend, and your torch shows a wooden doorway on your right. Will you open the door and slip through, hoping to evade your pursuers (turn to **46**), or continue on along the tunnel you are in (turn to **113**)?

150

Instead of a pass onto a trading ship Hardred produces a throwing dagger which is flying to your heart before you can even recognise it for what it is. He throws too quickly for it to be Hardred. Your prayer is answered in the nick of time. A glowing sphere of white light surrounds you, trapping the envenomed blade inches from your chest. You are held motionless but safe inside the circle of light and 'Hardred' curses and says, 'You have survived my attack this time, but I have never failed to kill my target. I shall hound you to your grave.' With that he turns to run. The light fades and you follow but the gardener with whom you exchanged pleasantries this morning emerges from behind the magnolia tree, blocking your way. On the steps of the temple the real Hardred beckons urgently. You run to him but he says, 'Gently, but yes, good news, a ship sails for Tor on the evening tide, I can vouch for the master.' You look around but the imposter has fled and the gardener is nowhere to be seen. Turn to 289.

151

As you deny his accusation, a yellow star bursts from his ring. Your Defence against it is 6 as it hurtles towards your chest. If you fail to dodge it, turn to 230. If you manage to evade it you may choose to attack him as he points the ring at you once more (turn to 290) or dive into the cloud of yellow gas, where he will not be able to see you (turn to 330).

152

The Hannya is too large to dodge the Shuriken easily and it lodges in one of her human arms. She screams in pain, the coils of her serpent body writhing. Instantly, you lash the ball of your foot at the slowed simian beast, in a Leaping Tiger kick. Because it is so slow you should be able to hit the O-Bakemono every time, but you must dodge its cumbersome return blow. You will also need to use a Shuriken on the Hannya each combat round to prevent it from using its sorcerous bolts, whilst it tries to avoid the throwing stars, until you have killed the O-Bakemono.

O-BAKEMONO
Defence against Leaping Tiger kick: 1
Endurance: 18
Damage: 2 dice

If you have killed the O-Bakemono you whirl to face the Hannya; turn to 390. If it is still alive, your

Defence against its enormous club is 10. If you have run out of Shuriken, bolts of green energy will bite into your side for every round the O-Bakemono stays alive and you will lose 3 Endurance each time. If you eventually kill it, and are not yourself killed in the process, turn to **390**.

153

You plunge into the chill, dark depths of the pool and swim to the back of the chamber. To your surprise, you locate an underwater tunnel ahead of you. Make a Fate Roll, but use only one die. If you score 1, 2, 3 or 4, turn to **80**. If you score a 5 or 6 turn to **332**.

154

Your leg flies towards the leader's head faster than lightning as you try to break his neck with the force of your Leaping Tiger kick.

BRIGAND LEADER
Defence against Leaping Tiger kick: 5
Endurance: 15
Damage: 1 Die + 2

If you win turn to **297**. If he still lives you must defend against his thrust (your Defence is 7), and against the cut of one of his men (your Defence is 6).

You may block only one. All of the brigands do the same damage as their leader when they hit. If you have attacked him four times and he still lives, turn to **337**. If not and if you still live, you may now punch (turn to **140**), throw (turn to **163**) or kick the leader again (return to the top of this paragraph).

155

As you glide down the tunnel which bends round some outjutting blocks of hard red rock, the cries of your pursuers ring hollowly behind you. As you round one particular red-coloured boulder, your training in the detection of traps sets off a mental alarm and you pull up short. Ahead is a dark greyish ooze – some kind of quicksand. You notice a slab of rock jutting slightly from the surface and you bound onto it, drops of grey sludge splattering your legs, and then over the ooze to the other side. You continue on your way, towards a large cavern. Before you reach it, you see a pool at the side of the tunnel. Will you hurry past it (turn to **72**), or use it to wash the grey filth from your garments (turn to **92**)?

156

As Mardolh's many arms sweep the air, claws extended, you turn away and then whip your leg round and up into the gruesome torso with all your power.

MARDOLH
Defence against Kwon's Flail: 6
Endurance: 30
Damage: 2 dice

If you win turn to **210**. If Mardolh still lives, he tries to rake your back before you can leap away. Your Defence is 7 and you may not block. If you survive his attack you may now use either the Leaping Tiger kick (turn to **166**), the Cobra Strike punch (turn to **207**), the Iron Fist (turn to **173**) or Kwon's Flail once more (return to the top of this paragraph).

157

As you force yourself to dwell upon what the Primordial Terror may do to you, the strain of what you have been through since you entered Quench-heart Keep begins to tell. Your sanity leaves you and you become a gibbering maniac, waiting for the nameless horror to engulf you in its ingesting embrace.

As the black, amorphous jelly flows around you and its juices eat at your skin, your heart fails you. At least the Scrolls of Kettsuin will be digested with you!

158

You spin and leap, punching and kicking but they are reckless and one sacrifices himself, hurling himself at you bodily. You kill him with a single blow but his body weighs you down and they overpower you. You are knocked against the coal bucket and your skull is smashed. They have regained the

Scrolls of Kettsuin and you lie dead in the slops and sawdust of the tavern floor.

159

You fall to the ground beside the steps with a jarring crunch, but you use your arms to break your fall somewhat, and only lose 2 Endurance. If you are still alive, you can see your assailant – surely another Ninja – swing nimbly into the pillared cloister of the boardwalk in front of the red and black lacquered doors. As you spring to your feet he turns and sends another Shuriken spinning towards you. You barely have enough time to bring your arm across and send the deadly throwing star ringing away with your Iron Sleeve. At the same time, your opponent darts through the doors. Turn to **195**.

160

You break the surface and the globe of air pops and is gone. As you swim west once more, under the hot sun, dark shadows circle beneath you. Plunging your head underneath the surface, you see three beings like manta rays with the heads of sharks. They are jackals of the deep, intelligent and evil. One swims head-on towards you. If you are skilled with Poison Needles turn to **279**. Otherwise you will have to try a Cobra Strike at its snout. Turn to **245**.

161

The bull-necked bodyguard lowers his head and shield-charges you, intent on throwing you back from the top of the staircase so that you can be surrounded. You must stop him at all costs. Will you try the Forked Lightning Strike (turn to **261**) or step aside and try to use the Tiger's Paw chop to the back of his neck as he charges past (turn to **288**)?

162

Are you a skilled Lock-pick? If you are, turn to **155**; if you are not turn to **141**.

163

Surprisingly, the three men before you move with military precision. The one on your left is a left-handed swordsman and while you try to parry the forceful blows of their leader and whirl him around your hip, the others attack from either side. The leader's Defence against your throw is 6. If you are successful, you use his body to block an incoming sword and he is pierced by the blade of one of his own men. Note that he loses 3 Endurance. There is no time to follow up with a killing blow. He rises to his feet as you parry another thrust. Will you punch (turn to **140**) or kick (turn to **154**)? If you fail, your side is cut and you lose 4 Endurance. If you are still alive, you may punch (turn to **140**) or kick (turn to **154**).

164

The goblins cry out in rage; you have trespassed in their sacred shrine. Two of them try to topple you over the edge. Make a Fate Roll. If Fate smiles on you, turn to **134**. If Fate turns her back on you, turn to **119**.

165

A minute passes in complete silence. As your eyes become accustomed to the gloom, you look over the top of the chest and around the room. Nothing. But you become convinced you can sense another presence in the room. Your questing gaze glances upwards and you freeze in surprise. A figure is clinging to the ceiling, using what you recognise to be Cat's Claws, the tools of the Ninja's Climbing skill. He is dressed as you are save for the curved and scabbarded sword or Ninjato, strapped to his back. He is still, except for his head which turns slowly. He too can sense you. Will you leap up and hurl a Shuriken at him (turn to 200) or, if you have any Flash Powder, you could pour it carefully onto the chest and use your flint and tinder to set it off, and then throw a Shuriken (turn to 260)?

166

Throwing caution to the wind you leap-kick and try to drive your heel into the unnatural horror's gaping maw, as it strikes with each of its arms in succession.

MARDOLH
Defence against Leaping Tiger kick: 8
Endurance: 30
Damage: 2 dice

If you win, turn to 210. If Mardolh still lives he tries to catch you and then dash you to the floor with all his godlike strength. Your Defence against him is 5. If you survive his attack you may now use the Iron Fist (turn to 173), the Cobra Strike punch (turn to 207) or if you have played AVENGER! and learnt this kick, Kwon's Flail (turn to 156).

167

With perfect judgement you whip your leg around and across behind your back, as you cling to the wall, and across the path of the bolt which smashes through a window to your right. The Cat's Claws begin to slip, furrowing the stone of the sheer wall and you are forced to twist your body through the broken glass of the window, before the Cat's Claws come away completely, and you cut yourself in the process. Lose 2 Endurance. Turn to **183**.

168

You are shown in to see Kiyamo and he listens quietly whilst you relate the night's events. When you have finished, he says, 'I am shamed that such a thing could have happened in my house. Thank Eo you are so formidable that I do not have the loss of your life on my conscience as well as that of Hizen and of the six guards.' You reply, 'Do not feel shamed, Lord. There was nothing you could have done in any case. He was Ninja.' He looks at you for a long moment and then shivers and drops his gaze. 'Yes, indeed.' There is a pause. Then he continues in a louder voice, 'Today you may travel to Iga – I shall send a force of five thousand men to accompany you. There is still much work to be done in the south. May Eo's blessings go with you!' You take your leave and a few hours later you and Gorobei are heading south. In two days' time you are at the port of Iga, on board a ship bound for the Island of Tranquil Dreams. Your spirit soars like a bird at the thought of home. Turn to **420**.

169

As you lash your foot out, first at his knee-cap and then at his face in quick succession, his cloak slips to reveal the red costume of a monk of the Scarlet Mantis. He seems to be unfamiliar with this kick and although he blocks the low kick, the higher one hits him full in the face and his neck snaps. Once more his head lolls inanely, this time in death. If you have not yet examined the contents of the strangely-shaped sack and wish to do so, turn to **361**. If you have already examined the sack or do not wish to, turn to **21**.

170

Your hand flies to your mouth and your assailants have no idea that you are about to blow a Poison Needle at one of them. Cassandra is too far away. Will you make the tall thief, Tyutchev, your target (turn to **391**) or try to embed the needle in the soft skin of Thaum (turn to **399**)?

171

You break into a run, and it rears up, roaring, arms flailing the air aggressively. As you near it you lean onto your left foot and use it as a pivot to spin to the right as, with incredible speed and a guttural scream, you call on your Inner Force. Your right leg is whipped around – it is a ball and chain; your foot is the ball, your leg the chain. The heel of your foot slams into the temple of the creature with a crack as your shout echoes around the clearing. The O-Bakemono drops, dead as a stone, its skull shattered and its brains pulped. Turn to **216**.

172

You are below the crest of the hill before the adventurers can stop you and are soon lost in woods. You press on through the hills until nightfall. If you have been through the caves of the goblins, turn to **213**. If not you spend a restful night below the stars. You may restore up to 2 points of lost Endurance. In the morning you climb another hill to see if you can catch sight of the Endless Sea, but it is far beyond the horizon. Will you head south-west, a way which looks rough and woody (turn to **44**), or due west where the land is more open and there is less cover (turn to **32**)?

173

Darting forward, you slam your fist towards the chest of the colossus as it bends over you, trying to gather you up in its many arms.

MARDOLH
Defence against Iron Fist: 8
Endurance: 30
Damage: 2 dice

If you win turn to **210**. If Mardolh still lives, your Defence against his grasping arms is 7. If you survive his attack you may now use either the Leaping Tiger kick (turn to **166**) or the Cobra Strike punch (turn to **207**), or if you have read Book 1: AVENGER! and learnt this kick, Kwon's Flail (turn to **156**).

174

A goblin, missings its legs and lower body, dangles at the foot of a plaited vine which is knotted round its neck. Its head is covered by a hood of purple leather which you know from your study of folklore denotes a goblin sacrifice to one of their gods. Below it is what looks like a pool of black, bubbling lava, twenty feet across. Its edges are distended into tongue-like legs and several pale green eyes quiver in the black jelly of its body. You are looking at a Primordial Terror: a relic from the days when every living thing on the world of Orb crept on its belly, long before the time of the Elder gods. As you stare in stupefied fascination, one of the green, lidless eyes floats into a tongue of matter which inches towards you. The Primordial Terror uses the Eldritch power of its thoughtless mind to hold you still until it can envelop you. You can think clearly even though you are rooted to the spot.

Will you try to spur yourself to action by dwelling on the grisly fate that awaits you (turn to **157**), force yourself to disbelieve in the apparition before you, knowing that if it is an illusion it will disappear (turn to **132**), recite the Ninja covenant, Ninja no Chigiri (turn to **115**) or if you have not done so already, will you call upon your god, Kwon the Redeemer, to be your salvation (turn to **99**)?

175

As you reach for a needle, Hardred produces a throwing dagger which is flying to your heart before you can even recognise it for what it is. He throws too quickly for it to be Hardred. If you have the skill of Arrow Cutting turn to **342**. If you do not, this is

128

the last thought you have as the dagger pierces your heart. The blade is grooved and covered in venom, but the steel alone has done its work. As you die 'Hardred' bows and says 'Mandrake, Guildmaster of Assassins, at your service, Ninja. Honoric will be pleased – for he still lives, Ninja, in spite of your efforts.' You have failed.

176

The stricken magician's words tumble over each other in a rush as he tells you that his friends are losing their blessed souls to the spirit of an undead Barbarian Warlord and that the spell he has mistakenly cast has made them helpless, unable to defend themselves. He looks sick with fear as he offers to give you something of rare magical power if you should spare him. Will you kill him with one blow and take his gleaming ring (turn to **204**), run to the help of his friends (turn to **397**) or help him to his feet and hold out your hand expectantly (turn to **128**)?

177

Make a Fate Roll:

If Fate smiles on you, turn to **272**.
If Fate turns her back on you, turn to **226**.

178

You give ground steadily and when one of the soldiers aims a cut at you you manage to turn the blade with a half block before it hits your side. You then collapse to the ground as if slain. You slow your breathing and metabolism immediately but, unfortunately, they decide to bury their swords in you as a matter of routine just to make sure, and they kill you in the process. The Scrolls of Kettsuin will never be returned to the Temple of the Rock now.

179

Ulrik's Haven is soon far behind you, as you travel south and then west across the wild terrain towards Wargrave Abbas. Turn to **131**.

180

You steal into the shadows of the cavern as the O-Bakemono rises to its feet. Suddenly you dash from the darkness and plunge the dagger into its back, driving it deep into its vitals. It stiffens and roars in pain, whirling around to face you, almost tearing the dagger from your grasp. It is still alive, although weakened by the poison and the wound. The young girl screams with wild hope. The lumbering beast has the strength to swing its club at you. You dodge the clumsy blow easily but several pulses of green energy fly from the fingers of the Hannya, exploding into your side. Lose 3 Endurance.

If you are still alive, will you throw some Flash Powder into the fire, if you have any, and drive a Winged Horse kick at the O-Bakemono's temple (turn to **112**), spit a Poison Needle at the O-Bakemono if you have that skill (turn to **139**) or hurl a Shuriken at the Hannya, whilst you try to finish off the O-Bakemono (turn to **152**)?

181

You somersault over the heads of the short crook-legged goblins and knock two to the floor before running on down the tunnel, deeper into the mountain. Turn to **149**.

182

You flip over in the air to land safely on your feet beside the steps of the guest house. Your assailant – surely another Ninja – swings nimbly into the pillared cloister of the boardwalk in front of the red and black lacquered doors. He turns and sends another Shuriken spinning towards you. You barely have enough time to bring your arm across and send the deadly throwing star ringing away with your Iron Sleeve. At the same time, your opponent darts through the doors. Turn to **195**.

183

When you have smashed your way through the window you find yourself in a deserted bedchamber with a door which opens out on the spiral staircase; this leads to the bottom of the Keep. As you glide down it you hear the clatter of guards coming down from the roof behind you, and a bugle which blows five sharp notes. You reach the hallway and the clank of armour alerts you as soldiers appear at both ends of the hall, but there is a doorway ahead of you. If you have played AVENGER!, did you kill the Keep's torturer in the torture chamber? If you did, turn to **302**. If you did not or have not played AVENGER!, turn to **314**.

184

As you descend, the tunnel spirals in ever-tighter circles. As you approach a blank wall at its end you notice a wide crack in the ceiling. Using your Ninja training and your skills as a detector of traps you examine the floor of the tunnel directly below it. Tell-tale cracks and worn holes show that spikes of some sort can descend from the roof; they would trap you if you went any further so you decide to go back to the main tunnel and continue your search for a way out of the mountain there. Turn to **76**.

185

You step closer. It rears up and roars, arms flailing the air aggressively. You place a needle on your tongue and spit vigorously. The needle hits the creature on its upper arm. The O-Bakemono claps its hand over the wound and roars in pain. It turns to you and scoops up its club. You stare, expecting it to topple but it remains unaffected and hurls its great club at you. This catches you by surprise and you are not quite quick enough in throwing yourself aside – the club grazes your hip, spinning you around with a sharp bruising pain. Lose 3 Endurance. If you are still alive, you see the huge beast falter slightly, a puzzled expression on its face, before it gives a bellowing shout and lumbers towards you, mouth wide, yellowed tusks of teeth bared. Quickly, you spit another needle at the creature. It roars in pain and staggers again; you spit once more and the O-Bakemono falls to its knees and then onto its face in the grass. It has taken enough venom for six men. Turn to **216**.

186

As the quarrel fired by the guard hums over your head, two more discharge from a trap in the wall, but you chop both hands across their path and the bolts hurtle into the walls on either side of you. You rush on through the door. Turn to **271**.

187

Tyutchev wields the massive two-handed sword negligently in one hand and he whirls the blade in an arc, smashing your speeding throwing star aside with breathtaking ease. It clatters against the cellar wall. Thaum finishes his spell and producing a brass horn, inlaid with mother of pearl, from within his voluminous robes he pours a river of steaming acid towards you, as Tyutchev leaps aside. The acid sprays towards you, like a geyser. Will you roll to the ground, hoping it will pass above you (turn to **202**) or let it hit you and attack regardless (turn to **227**)?

188

You run quickly to the rough-hewn block of stone and in the light of your torch you can make something out, carved into the grey rock. It looks like an amoeboid mass of jelly and globe-like tentacles, with many eyes floating in the body of the being. The carving is crude but the likeness is enough to suggest something truly hideous and the eyes seem to claim your attention as you strain to see if one of them is moving to look at you. Your scalp crawls. The carvings beneath it show that what must be goblins are sacrificing their own people to it, in the absence of victims of other races. The evil fascination which the altar exercises over your spirit is broken as two goblins clad in greasy leather aprons walk into the cave. They cry out and run back up the tunnel and you decide to continue on your way, down the opposite tunnel which leads deeper into the mountains. Turn to **149**.

189

Your body craves oxygen and the Garotte bites into your throat. You will be dead in moments. Lose 2 Endurance. If you are still alive, you calm yourself and slip into a deep meditative trance, calling on your years of training, to slow your heartbeat down. Sinking into a kind of suspended animation, your body slumps as if dead – even your skin holds the grey pallor of death. A few moments later you can dimly sense a shout of triumph and the constriction around your neck is gone. As if from far away, you can feel someone rifling through your clothes; the Ninja is looking for the Scrolls of Kettsuin. It seems those who follow the Way of the Scorpion know nothing of the deathlike trance of the Ninja from the Island of Tranquil Dreams. Choosing your moment you surge up and out of the trance, eyes flicking open, lungs gulping air. Your assailant is kneeling over you, his appearance similar to yours, save for his glittering black eyes and the scabbarded sword or Ninjato, strapped to his back. His head turns to you, eyes wide and staring in shock and surprise. You drive an Iron Fist at his head, putting the power of your body behind the blow as you sit up. It smashes into his face and he flies backwards, but he rolls with the blow and comes to his feet some distance away as you leap up. You may note that he has lost 3 Endurance. With a shout he reaches up and draws his sword with both hands in one incredibly swift motion. He stands, presenting only the side of his body to you, right foot forward, left knee bent and at right angles to his body, sword-hip pointing up at your throat, arms extended. Gingerly, you massage your throat, as the pair of you circle each other, warily. Turn to **22**.

190

The look of surprise on the goblin riders' faces is comical as you jump high into the air, and somersault above the stone tips of their lances, to land behind them. They whirl their agile mounts and turn to the attack once more. Turn to **246**.

191

Your opponent shouts, 'Can you withstand the poison of the Spiderfish again, Ninja?' As he does so, you take the chance to wrap your arms around him, so he cannot strike, knowing you will be at a disadvantage for a few moments if you can withstand the force of the venom once more. Desperately you cling on as, cursing, he tries to shake you off, whilst waves of nausea and pain consume you. It is much worse this time. Lose 2 Endurance. If you are still alive, it passes, leaving you weak and sweating. With a strength borne of desperation, you manage to trip the other Ninja – it seems he has neglected his training somewhat in hand-to-hand combat in favour of the sword. You stagger back, taking a brief respite to regain your equilibrium as he springs to his feet. Your years of training to withstand extreme hardship and virulent poison have served you well. He is up but you can attack again. Will you try a Forked Lightning Strike kick (turn to **55**), a Tiger's Paw chop (turn to **304**) or try the Whirlpool Throw once more (turn to **87**)?

192

You back slowly away towards the glowing coals of the brazier as the soldiers pour onto the roof and begin to circle you warily. The rain has stopped but the wind still moans around the turrets of the Keep. You cast your handful of Flash Powder into the coals. (Cross it off your Character Sheet.) You shield your eyes as the powder ignites, its flash more brilliant than lightning in the moonless night. The soldiers are unable to see in the darkness and you slip between them with the grace of a black panther and glide down the staircase of the Great Keep to the hallway below. The clatter of armour and clink of mailed feet alerts you as soldiers run towards you from both ends of the hall, but there is a doorway ahead of you. Did you kill the Keep's torturer in AVENGER!? If you did, turn to **302**. If you did not or have not played AVENGER!, turn to **314**.

193

Each day you climb a headland to stare down at the ships which sail past towards the harbour. Your heart yearns for the Island of Tranquil Dreams and the safe fulfilment of your mission. When the second tenday is almost up you at last catch sight of a large three masted sailing ship, its three square sails billowing in the wind which drives in from the sea. You make your way to the harbour the next day to find the *Sack of the South* preparing to set sail once more for Upanishad, a great city far to the south. You board the ship. Turn to **406**.

194

You flee just in time as a band of monks of the Scarlet Mantis give chase. There are too many of them to defeat and they drive you towards a group of hunting dogs which you guess are from Quench-heart Keep. You can outrun the men, but the dogs are still on your trail as you climb into the Goblin's Teeth Mountains hoping to climb a ledge which they cannot and then escape west over the other side of the mountains. But you are at the end of your tether now, utterly exhausted. Lose 2 Endurance. If you are still alive, turn to **336**.

195

As quickly as you can, you leap the stairs and into the guest house. Whirling away from the entrance and the illuminating moonlight, into the shadows you stop, controlling your breathing. Everything is quiet and there is no sign of the other Ninja. The sliding doors are still. There is no hint of recent movement. He is probably still in the room. Your eyes strain to pierce the gloom. Suddenly, he shoots up from behind a chest, the all-too-familiar bamboo blowpipe at his lips, and there is a woosh of exhaled air. Make a Block Roll. Your Defence is 7 for this roll. If you succeed, turn to **205**. If you fail, turn to **218**.

196

As the quarrel fired by the guard hums over your head, two more discharge from a trap in the wall and one of them pierces your windpipe. You sink gurgling to the floor and your lungs fill with blood. You drown in your own life-blood in the hallway of Quench-heart Keep.

197

Suddenly, you rip the canvas open and leap into the tent, to be greeted with gasps of amazement. With blurring speed you send a Shuriken spinning towards Akira. It rips into his throat, tearing it open and he keels over backwards, gurgling horribly as blood fountains from his neck. He is dead within moments. Jikkyu's face is a mask of astonishment mixed with a trace of fear as he spits out one word, full of malice and hate, 'Ninja!' Turn to **338**.

198

Your throwing star whirrs from your hand and embeds itself in the magician's arm; he falls to the damp floor of the cellar, his spell lost. But he is soon struggling to his feet again. Incidentally, your natural cunning, cleverly attacking the magician before he could cast his spell, will stand you in good stead if you live. You may add one to the Attack Modifier of your choice. Thaum props himself up, looking at the blood that is forming a large brown patch on his robes. Cassandra cries out in rage, as Tyutchev turns to help the fallen magician, and she advances quickly to the attack. Turn to **121**.

199

You run quickly to the rough-hewn block of stone and in the light of your torch you can make something out, carved into the grey rock. It looks like an amoeboid mass of jelly with globe-like tentacles, and many eyes floating in its body. The carving is crude but the likeness is enough to suggest something truly hideous and the eyes seem to claim your attention as you strain to see if one of them is moving to look at you. Your scalp crawls. The carvings beneath it show that goblins sacrifice their own people to it, in the absence of victims of other races. The evil fascination which the altar exercises over your spirit is broken by the raucous cries of goblins. Twenty or so of them, clad in greasy, black leather armour and brandishing short, stabbing swords, are running at you. If you are a skilled Acrobat turn to **181**. If you are not, you must fight them with your back to the precipice. Turn to **164**.

200

You jump up. The figure looks at you and tries to move across the roof, almost leaping from one point to another as your hand blurs through the air, sending a Shuriken hurtling towards him. Make a Shuriken Roll. His Defence is 6 as he attempts to dodge. If you hit him, turn to **239**. If you fail, turn to **250**.

201

You run as fast as you can – your Ninja training in woodcraft enabling you to cover your own tracks Soon you lose sight of your pursuers and you head for the valley of the River Crow. Turn to **135**.

202

The acid curves downward magically, like a striking

water serpent, and you are bathed from head to foot. The pain is excruciating; it feels as if all of your flesh is being stripped away. You writhe in agony, but Tyutchev steps into the pool of acid, apparently unconcerned and the realisation that you have been tricked by an illusion comes too late. Tyutchev buries his sword in your back and pierces through to your heart. They will use the knowledge contained in the Scrolls of Kettsuin to spread chaos across Orb.

203

Make a Shuriken Roll. The first goblin rider's Defence against your throwing star is 6 as he tries to catch it on his small round shield of boiled leather. If you hit him you may note that his Endurance is reduced by 3. His makeshift lance dips to the ground, but your Defence as you try to knock the second lance aside is 6 for the other goblin rider is already upon you. If you fail, the impact throws you backwards and you lose 6 Endurance. If you are still alive you give battle. Turn to 246.

204

Your fist chops down into his jugular vein and the shock kills the young magician. You thrust the gleaming Sun-Star ring onto your finger and race away down the hillside, just as the priest in white staggers coughing out of the yellow fog. He is in no condition to chase you and you make good your escape across the rolling wolds towards the Crow river. Turn to 144.

205

Instantly you throw yourself aside and a small feathered dart flies into the wall behind you. Your nostrils flare as you recognise the acrid smell of Spiderfish venom. The other Ninja jumps up and over the chest to land nimbly some feet before you. With a shout he reaches up and draws his sword with both hands in one incredibly swift motion. He stands, presenting only the side of his body to you, right foot forward, left knee bent and at right angles to his body, sword-hip pointing up at your throat, arms extended. You begin to circle each other warily. Turn to **22**.

206

You kill four of your assailants with bone-crushing kicks and punches but soon you are surrounded and one of them manages to club you unconscious from behind with a war-hammer. You begin to regain your senses as they are carrying you into the dank darkness of the Keep's torture chamber. They bind you with ropes while a set of manacles are heated in a small furnace. Are you are skilled Escapologist? If you are turn to **328**. If you are not, turn to **344**.

207

The waving of Mardolh's four arms is fascinatingly and disturbingly bizarre as he claws the air questing for your fragile body. You give ground, then lunge quickly with a Cobra Strike jab.

MARDOLH
Defence against Cobra Strike: 7
Endurance: 30
Damage: 2 dice

If you win turn to **210**. If Mardolh still lives your

Defence against his questing arms is 6. If you survive his attack you may now use either the Leaping Tiger kick (turn to **166**), the Iron Fist (turn to **173**) or Cobra Strike again (return to the top of this paragraph), or if you have played AVENGER! and learnt this kick, Kwon's Flail (turn to **156**).

208
You are no match for the creatures of the deep, being clumsy and slow in the water by comparison. The Narwhal dips its sharp horn just before you grab it and its enormous momentum drives it right through your body, killing you instantly. The Scrolls of Kettsuin are lost forever.

209
Your throwing star whistles through the air, but Cassandra dodges; she has the reflexes of a panther and she bounds to the attack as your star buries itself in the oaken panel of the door which she bolted behind you. Tyutchev and Thaum start to close in on you. Turn to **121**.

210
You have defeated Mardolh, a Greater Son of Nil. He is not dead, but as you prepare to attack again his form seems to crumble. Parts of his very being drop away, dissolving to nothing before they hit the floor. Each crumbling piece leaves behind a blackness so deep that it is almost blinding. Mardolh is returning, piece by piece, to the Void, and the Void has come to Orb. Soon there is no trace of the unnatural fiend save a statue of absolute nothing-

ness, a black gateway to the Void. You have unwittingly opened a doorway from the Void to Orb, but there is nothing you can do about it now. Something moves in the darkness of the subterranean precincts of the temple and you decide to abandon any thoughts of reward from the priestesses of Illustra. One who has mastered the Way of the Tiger has no use for gold other than to give it to the poor. A gobbet of black poison is all that remains of Mardolh, the most virulent poison of all, Blood of Nil. You gingerly scrape it from the floor into a small glass phial. Note this on your Character Sheet. Then you turn back to the oak-panelled doorway and manage, at last, to open it, finding one of Cassandra's daggers which she had used to wedge it shut as you do so. You slip it into your pack and walk warily up the staircase. Turn to **395**.

211

Using your ability to Feign Death so that even your body goes rigid and cold, you concentrate your mind to slow your metabolism. This also means that you can go without oxygen for abnormally long periods. You are dimly aware that the Moat Horror drags you ever deeper and then up again into a water-filled cave. When your body has gone cold it lets you free of the suckered folds of its rubbery skin and you feel the movement of water in the cave as it floats back into the moat, but you sense that it still lurks nearby. With a small effort of will you cause your heart to beat normally once more and you then reach out and feel the ceiling of the water-filled cave. It is thick clay and you scrabble feverishly at it, your lungs bursting, until at last you have made a small hole through which air can reach you. Within minutes you have enlarged it sufficiently to allow you to squeeze through onto the grass above. The

Moat Horror's cave was just below the ground at the far edge of the moat and you have escaped from Quench-heart Keep, at least for the moment. As you lie panting in the darkness, you hear the baying of bloodhounds and the yap of wardogs. They are hunting you! Will you:

Run towards the Goblin's Teeth Mountains that tower before you (turn to 336)?

Run south towards the Sea of the Star (turn to 362)?

Or circle Quench-heart Keep and head for the City of Druath Glennan (turn to 409)?

212

Cautiously but quickly you slide the door open, step through, slide it shut and spin into the shadows beside the door in one movement. It is deathly quiet and as black as coal. Your every sense is straining to pick up any sight, sound or smell as you stand, as quiet as the grave and as still as a stone, the nape of your neck tingling as you begin to sense another presence in the room. As your eyes become accustomed to the gloom you look up to see a figure clinging to the ceiling. The sight makes you start in surprise and you recognise Cat's Claws, spiked clamps used in the Climbing skill of the Ninja. Suddenly the figure drops from the ceiling. He is dressed as you are, save for a curved scabbarded sword or Ninjato, strapped to his back. As he drops, his hand flickers in and then out, and a Shuriken, almost identical to your own, whirrs through the air towards you. Do you have the skill of Arrow Cutting? If you do, turn to 285. If you do not, turn to 296.

213

When you awake in the morning your body is

covered in black swellings. You have caught the plague in the caves of the goblins and you slip into a raging fever and delirium. You dream that you are helpless, outside the gates of the Temple of the Rock, on the Island of Tranquil Dreams, surrounded by all the foes you have killed. For three days and nights you are close to death and when the fever finally breaks you are weak and your limbs tremble. Subtract 1 from your Kick Modifier; in the fever you have lost your strength. You rest again and then climb another hill to see if you can catch sight of the Endless Sea, but it is beyond the horizon. Will you head south-west, a way which looks rough and woody (turn to **44**), or due west where the land is more open and there is less cover (turn to **32**)?

214

Suddenly, you rip the canvas open and leap into the tent, to be greeted with gasps of astonishment. You have a needle on your tongue and you shoot it towards Akira in a flash. It pierces his throat and his eyes widen in surprise and glaze over as the venom takes effect. He slumps to the floor, jerking spasmodically. Jikkyu's face is a mask of astonishment, mixed with a trace of fear, as he spits out one word, full of hate and malice, 'Ninja!' Turn to **338**.

215

You point the sword at them and let it go, hoping that it will attack your foes, but it falls point-first on the floor and is grasped by one of the goblins. You decide to leave the sword to them as you cannot use it and make a break for the next cavern. Go to **237**.

216

At least it will never terrorise the villagers any more. You look around for further tracks but all you find are a series of the same well-worn tracks of the O-Bakemono leading right up to the rock-face as if they carried on right through. You also notice that beside the clawed feet of the O-Bakemono the grass has been scorched, and fluted grooves some two feet wide have been left in the earth as if something heavy and tubular had been dragged along it, also disappearing into the rock. You feel up and down the rock-face, pushing and testing for a secret door or hidden entrance. Eventually, you find a hair-like crack and you are able to make out a door in the rock-face. Then you notice a small carved glyph in the rock. Excitedly, you trace the symbol with your finger and the door begins to rumble open. Suddenly there is a flash – your reflexes are as quick as the strike of the Praying Mantis; you flip backwards but a great ball of orange flame billows out of the glyph and you are caught at its edges, before it burns out and is gone. Anyone else would have been completely consumed. As it is, you are badly injured. Lose 3 Endurance. If you are still alive, a cave mouth yawns before you. You walk into it and it narrows to a winding corridor lit with torches. Turn to **293**.

217

Your kick floors the young magician and you land beside his prostrate form, poised to give the killing blow. His mottled cloak, the colour of autumn leaves with five cloth-of-gold arrows pointing out from a central hub, hides the sorcerous oddities which he uses when concocting spells. But it will be the work of a moment to kill him and steal the gleaming Sun-Star ring. If this is what you wish to do, turn to **204**. Or you may wish to ask him again what is happening as he lies helpless, warning him that to attempt a spell would mean death (turn to **176**).

218

A small dart jabs into the flesh just between your eyes before you can move. Do you have Immunity to Poisons? If you have, turn to **244**. If you have not, turn to **256**.

219

The soldier cuts at you with his long sword. Your Defence as you try to flip backwards out of range is 9. After his blow (and if you are still alive) you can close in and use the Tiger's Paw chop (turn to **233**) or the Winged Horse kick (turn to **101**).

220

Just past a sharp bend in the tunnel, your spluttering torch shows a wooden door in the right hand wall. You check it for traps before opening it gently. A tunnel leads steeply down, curving sharply to the left. The air in this tunnel is dank and there is no movement in it. Will you investigate it (turn to **90**) or continue along the tunnel you are in (turn to **76**)?

221

Taking the Water Crystal which the prince of the Sea-Elves gave to you for helping to save him from the Sea-Jackals, you cast it to the floor at your feet. It shatters leaving a small blue drop on the damp floor which swells until a huge watery figure, like a breaking tidal wave, towers above you. You order it to attack Mardolh and it rolls forward and slams into the colossal fiend like a storm-wave breaking against a cliff. The cellar shakes and Mardolh shudders, but its four arms flail powerfully at the water elemental. The battle rages for some time but you can see that the Son of Nil is too strong for the elemental. At last its essence is scattered like so many raindrops across the floor and walls. Mardolh turns to you. You will have to rely on your martial arts; turn to **301**, but note that Mardolh is severely weakened after the titanic struggle. Its scorpion tail droops uselessly and the horror has lost 14 Endurance.

222
You decide to leave the disgustingly bloated purple air-sac alone and continue on your way. Turn to **21**.

223
The Narwhal turns aside at the last moment and you catch sight of a crystal dagger buried in its back, close to its blow-hole. You catch one of its fins and pull yourself onto its back as it hurtles through the sea at amazing speed. You pull out the dagger and it falls to the bottom. The whale swims on, either happy to tow you or oblivious of your presence. The merman is soon lost behind you in the green haze of the deep. Turn to **264**.

224
In the morning you sit cross-legged in the cowshed, meditating on the success of your mission so far, thankful that you have at last reached a tributary of the Endless Sea. You must decide whether to wait twenty days for the *Sack of the South*, the barbarian overlord's merchantman, or try your luck at Wargrave Abbas. If you decide to stay, turn to **193**. If you set out for Wargrave, turn to **179**.

225

You are still high above the courtyard when two more crossbow bolts slam into you, one hitting your leg, the other your wrist. You lose your grip on the sheer wall and plummet to your death.

226

You wait, poised to strike anything that comes through the door, quiet as a mouse, your spine tingling and your breathing soundless and shallow. There is no sound other than the light tinkle of the courtyard fountain and the chirruping of the crickets. Suddenly there is a tearing sound behind you. You step forward but the blade of a sword rips through the wall and slides across the side of your ribs, parting the flesh and drawing blood. Lose 3 Endurance. If you are still alive, you gasp in pain and whirl. For a brief moment the blade seems to shimmer like water, laced with ribbons of black in the creamy moonlight, and it is gone. Will you jump up and climb onto the roof surrounding the inner courtyard (turn to 334), open the door and roll into the room beyond (turn to 322) or drive a Winged Horse kick through the wall, now stained with your blood, approximately one foot above the hole (turn to 308)?

227

You do not even feel the acid as it appears to splash against you; it was merely an illusion. You strike at Tyutchev, but the magical black cloak which he wears makes him appear to be closer than he really is and you miss as he steps back, quick as a cat. You spin round as Cassandra almost buries her sword in your back and attack her instead. Turn to **121**.

228

The first goblin tries to spit you with his lance. Your Defence is 6 as you try to knock it aside, the second goblin close behind the first. If you fail, the impact throws you backwards and you lose 6 Endurance. If you are still alive, or if you successfully avoided the lance, you give battle. Turn to **246**.

229

One of the guards frowns in thought at this and then tells you to wait whilst he goes inside. A tense moment passes and then he comes out and nods with a curt, 'In you go then.' You step into the tent. It is large and spacious, lit by several lanterns and littered with the paraphernalia of a commander on the march. Two men are poring over a large map on a table. One is big and bulky, arrogantly handsome, the other tall and lean, a curiously shaped longbow slung on his back. They look up briefly and the handsome man says, 'One moment,' in a rich mellow voice and then turns to his companion, 'No, Akira, it must be the pass.' The other replies, 'But surely, my lord Jikkyu, Kiyamo will be expecting that.' And so the discussion goes on.

Will you hurl a Shuriken at Jikkyu (turn to **259**), spit a Poisoned Needle, if you have that skill, at Jikkyu (turn to **269**) or wait for a better opportunity – perhaps Akira will leave the room (turn to **282**)?

230

The yellow ball explodes against your chest with the power of an Iron Fist with Inner Force. Lose 9 Endurance. If you are still alive, will you attack him as he points the ring at you once more (turn to **290**), or dive into the cloud of yellow gas where he will not be able to see you (turn to **330**)?

231

You point the ring at the horror from the Void and shout 'Rahelios!' The gleaming Sun-Star ring explodes in your face. Lose 4 Endurance. The magician must have told you the wrong magical word of command. But if you are still alive, you see that a Sun-Star has erupted from the ring as you intended and blasted a great hole in Mardolh's chest and withered his scorpion tail. The unnatural fiend bellows deafeningly and towers over you. You will have to rely now on your martial arts. Turn to **301**, but note that Mardolh's Endurance is reduced by 12.

232

You surprise Cassandra by sliding feet first across the floor and your legs scythe the panther-like warrior-woman to the ground. As she tries to twist aside you roll on top of her, pinning her to the cold floor of the cellar, and drive your fist into the side of her head. She screams and goes rigid. You roll away and leap to your feet as Tyutchev attacks. Turn to **281**.

233

The Keep guard lunges with his sword once again as

you use the advantage of your higher position to chop the side of your palm down at his neck.

KEEP GUARD
Defence against Tiger's Paw chop: 5
Endurance: 12
Damage: 1 die

If you have killed the Keep guard turn to **249**. Otherwise you must try to dodge the tip of his long sword. Your Defence is 8. If you are still alive, you may use the Winged Horse kick (turn to **101**) or the Tiger's Paw chop (return to the top of this paragraph).

234

As you settle down to sleep the opal ring on your finger begins to glow. You look and the opal seems to grow until it fills the whole of your vision. It clears as if a mist had been blown out of it and the hatchet-face of Ulrik Skarsang's adviser appears, a black whirlpool painted on his right cheek. His brow is furrowed with effort and his eyes dart questingly to left and right. 'Where are you stranger?' you hear. 'Why can I not see you – the Chalice of Visions should show you to me. You must be the one, the killer of Manse the Deathmage, where are you?' At length he gives up and the opal is opaque once more. With a shock you realise that the adviser reveres Nemesis and you resolve to pass the night hidden between rocks, beyond a headland. The morning dawns bright and breezy. You must decide whether to wait twenty days for the *Sack of the South*, the barbarian overlord's merchantman, or to try your luck at Wargrave Abbas. If you decide to stay, turn to **193**. If you decide to set out for Wargrave, turn to **179**.

235

You put several miles between yourself and the Goblin's Teeth Mountains before pausing to rest after the rigours you have endured. You are awakened from a deep sleep lasting a day and a night by light rain falling. It is the beginning of a beautiful summer's day. You may restore up to 4 points of lost Endurance. The Sea of the Star glitters in the occasional sunlight of the south and you decide to continue west to the shore of the Endless Sea so that you may avoid crossing the Manmarch where you now have many foes. The only beings of any interest that you espy are a few stocky mountain dwarves, like small specks, on a far-away hilltop. After two days' travel you leave the woodlands behind and climb towards a line of conical hills. Towards the end of the day an itching in your armpits becomes acute and you notice unpleasant black swellings all over your chest. There is nothing you can do but travel on. Turn to **415**.

236

With your last vestige of free will you sink into the meditative trance of the Ninjas of the Island of Tranquil Dreams, used to slow the body's metabolism. Your mind slips out of the physical world and you can no longer be affected by hypnotic magic. Dimly, you hear a screech of frustration and hate. Then you can feel a faint touch on your leg, curiously hot. Instantly, you rush up to consciousness. Turn to **287**.

237

You run on once more, legs heavy with fatigue, and you have put two sharp twists of the tunnel behind you when you come to a passage-way, at the foot of some crudely carved steps on your right, which leads into darkness. You pause to take stock, but another group of goblins appears above you on the steps. Not stopping to think, other than to wish that the misshapen and spiteful goblins had never been created, you take the way that leads into darkness. It seems to turn back on itself and plunges downhill sharply, but by now you are utterly confused by the labyrinthine windings of the goblin tunnels. You have gone very deep below the mountain-side before you realise that there are no sounds of pursuit. Turning a corner your torch half lights a repellent and terrifying sight. Turn to **174**.

238

If you know for sure what type of creatures lives in these caves, turn to **199**. If you are not yet sure, turn to **188**.

239

Your Shuriken slams into his shoulder and he grunts in pain. His shoulder gives way and he comes away from the ceiling falling, but he flips in mid-air and plucks the Shuriken from his back as his feet hit the ground. At almost the same instant he sends it flying back at you. You duck, there is a whirr as it streaks over your head, followed by a crisp, tearing sound as it goes on and out through the paper-thin wall into the courtyard. There is a pause as you both stare at each other, the insistent flutter of shreds of the torn wall in a sudden night breeze echoing the flurry of explosive violence. You may note that he has lost 3 Endurance for your Shuriken. With a shout he reaches up and draws his sword with both hands in one incredibly swift motion. He stands, presenting only the side of his body to you, right foot forward, left knee bent and at right angles to his body, sword-hip pointing up at your throat, arms extended. You begin to circle each other warily. Turn to **22**.

240

You prise yourself free from the vicious barb, but the poison is so virulent it attacks your heart. Lose 5 Endurance. If you are still alive you may fight on. Turn to **301**.

241

The young magician's eyes narrow. He looks at your black Ninja costume. 'I would never give the Sun-Star jewel to one who worships Torremalku the Slayer.' Torremalku you know to be the assassin's god. You tell him that you despise the followers of the Slayer. Turn to **151**.

242

One of them says, 'Wait here,' and disappears into the tent. A moment later an arrow hurtles out, taking you by surprise and sinking into your chest. You are thrown backwards and fall in a heap on the floor, your life's blood draining away. A tall and lean man with a curiously shaped bow steps out. 'I am Akira. What message did I give you, dog!?' he sneers. It is the last thing you ever hear.

243

You drive your fist into the skull of one of the wardogs, cracking it, but a second grabs your wrist in its jaws. As you try to shake it off you are knocked to the ground by another and your throat is torn out.

The bloodhounds wait until the wardogs have finished with your carcass, before eating their fill.

244

You recognise the acrid smell of Spiderfish venom but you know your body can overcome its ravages. Even so, a wave of pain and nausea comes over you and you stagger. In that moment, your opponent, with a quick exhalation of triumph, hurls a Shuriken. You desperately try to swing away from it but it thuds into your thigh. Lose 3 Endurance. If you are still alive, the nausea passes and you stand erect, plucking the Shuriken from your leg. The other Ninja starts in amazement, and then you can see understanding in his eyes, and hear a muted 'Of course,' spoken under his breath. With a shout he reaches up and draws his sword with both hands in one incredibly swift motion. He stands, presenting only the side of his body to you, right foot forward, left knee bent and at right angles to his body, sword-hip pointing up at your throat, arms extended. You begin to circle each other warily. Turn to **22**.

245

Your blow discourages the Sea-Jackal's attack but another clamps its jaws on your leg and shakes you like a rag doll. Your blood sends them mad and they tear viciously at you as you strike out vainly to protect yourself. You are no match for them in their own element as they tear you to shreds. The Scrolls of Kettsuin are lost forever.

246

Will you punch (turn to **258**), kick (turn to **273**) or try to topple one of the goblins from his mount by using a throw (turn to **299**)?

247

With desperate speed, you bathe the blade of Cassandra's dagger in the Blood of Nil taken from Mardolh. The Hannya's human arms desperately try to stop your blow but you care not where it lands and the blade gashes her upper arm. The effect is instantaneous. The Hannya screams wildly, a sound that seems to echo into the spiritual planes, and the coils go limp for a moment, allowing you to jump free before they constrict again in an awful jerking paroxysm as the Hannya dies. You step back from the steaming body and go over to the girl, releasing her from her chains. She is in a state of shock and you lead her back to the village and her family. At the sight of you and the girl the whole village runs out to meet you, shouting and screaming their thanks and joy. They beg you to stay for a celebration they plan for the evening in your honour, but you tell them you cannot. After a quick meal you set off again for the Palace of Lord Kiyamo, their blessings and thanks ringing in your ears as you leave. Turn to **350**.

Cassandra looks into your eyes, watching for the flicker that will betray your strike the moment before it comes. You lash your foot out at her kneecap and then at the side of her head but she recognises that the first attack is little more than a feint. Her sword shadows your attack and she moves with the speed of a panther, blocking you. Your leg is badly cut and stung by the cold of her sword. You lose 6 Endurance. If you are still alive, Tyutchev is now upon you and you try frenziedly to block their whirlwind attacks. It seems that sword points attack you from everywhere at once. They are so skilful it is as if you are fighting ten, not two. After a time, Tyutchev feints a slash and reverses the angle of his blow, chopping into your hip. Your Defence against this skilful attack is only 6 and you may not block. If you fail, a gout of blood wells from your side. Lose 7 Endurance. If you are still alive you may Feign Death, if you have the skill (turn to **317**) or continue to defend yourself as best you can (turn to **331**).

The Keep guard's neck breaks with a satisfying crack and his body tumbles down the staircase like a rag doll and is trampled underfoot by a great mountain of a man, the Bailiff's bodyguard, who strides up the staircase to do battle. Will you sprint across the roof of the Keep and try an enormous leap, hoping to clear the castle wall and land in the moat far below (turn to **34**) or stay to do battle (turn to **161**)?

Just as the figure, surely another Ninja, slams his Cat's Claws into the ceiling, your Shuriken thuds into the soft plaster where he was a moment ago.

Suddenly, the figure drops from the ceiling and as he turns in mid-air his hand flickers in and out and a Shuriken, almost identical to your own, whirrs through the air towards you. The figure lands on his feet, with a soft exhalation of breath. Have you the skill of Arrow Cutting? If you have, turn to **285**. If you have not, turn to **296**.

251

You lash out at the unnatural beast, hurting it, but the four arms grab at you and the giant scorpion tail darts forward, embedding its barb in your shoulder. The black venom which it injects is the Blood of Nil, the most virulent of poisons. If you are immune to poisons through training, turn to **240**. If not, death is almost instantaneous. You have been vanquished by Mardolh, a Son of Nil, one of the most powerful denizens of Orb.

252

The tunnel bends downwards and a set of steps leads on ahead. You hurry down them into a cave with a great square of rough-hewn rock at its centre. Beyond the rock is a precipice, so deep that your torch cannot light its bottom. A tunnel leads on beyond the cave. If you wish to examine the rock, turn to **238**. If you would rather hurry past the precipice turn to **220**.

253

The Goblin King collapses, limbs splayed, and the Dancing Sword clatters to the floor. You pick it up as the cave is suddenly filled by maddened goblins.

Will you run on into the next cavern (turn to **237**) or try to use the Dancing Sword against them (turn to **215**)?

254

Cassandra looks into your eyes, watching for the flicker that will betray your strike the moment before it comes. Your fist snaps towards her temple and the tip of her sword whirrs upwards to knock your arm aside. She has the reactions of a panther and her Defence against your Iron Fist punch is 8. If you hit her the power of your blow knocks her senseless and she collapses like a sack of coal (turn to **281**) as Tyutchev now attacks you. If she blocks your blow the speed of her riposte defies belief as she cuts open your jerkin from collar to belly. Lose 5 Endurance as the cold fire of her rune sword sears you. If you are still alive you may Feign Death, if you have the skill (turn to **317**), or continue to defend yourself as best you can (turn to **331**).

255

As you duck, a flagstone settles beneath your foot and there is a click from the wall to your left. Do you have the skill of Arrow Cutting? If you do, turn to **186**. If you do not, turn to **196**.

256

To your horror, you recognise the acrid smell of Spiderfish venom. Strangely, the knowledge of certain death lends you a serene calm. The poison courses through you, and you sink to your knees, jerking spasmodically, waiting quietly for the end. Through the burning agony, you hear the approaching footsteps of your opponent and his words, 'I am Ninja. I follow the Way of the Scorpion. So it is proven that the Way of the Scorpion overshadows the Way of the Tiger just as the power of Nemesis overshadows that of Kwon. But you have met Death with honour and so I shall ease your journey on that road.' With that, he strikes your head from your shoulders with one cut of his sword. At least you have not suffered the painful death of the Spiderfish.

257

The young magician hesitates, then says, 'Get back. You are an assassin, or er-well, I'm not carrying any poison, I'm a th-th-thaumaturgist, what need have I? I've no quarrel with a follower of Torremalku the Slayer, er-the Great!' He smiles weakly at you, then points the ring once more in your direction. Torremalku the Slayer you know to be the assassin god. Will you tell him that you worship Kwon, the Redeemer (turn to 266), say that you are no assassin (turn to 151) or attack him before he can cast a spell (turn to 290)?

258

The goblins are now using short, stabbing swords as

their mounts try to embed their enormous incisors into your legs. You lean over one of the giant rats and lash out with an Iron Fist punch. You may choose which goblin or giant rat to attack but, beware, these goblins are cunning fighters.

	1st GOBLIN RIDER	2nd GOBLIN RIDER	1st GIANT RAT	2nd GIANT RAT
Endurance:	7	8	9	9
Defence:	6	6	5	5
Damage:	1 die	1 die	1 die	1 die

If you are able to defeat them all, turn to **313**. If three or four are still alive, your Defence against their attacks is 6. If, as you dodge and duck, there are fewer than this, your Defence is 8. Each has an individual attack and you may only Block one of them. If you survive, you may punch again (return to the top of this paragraph) or kick (turn to **273**).

259

With blurring speed you hurl a Shuriken at Jikkyu's throat. Your throw is accurate but somehow, incredibly, it has little effect, leaving only a slight gash to mark its passage. In a moment Akira has an arrow ready in his bow and Jikkyu has shouted for the guards. You manage to avoid Akira's first arrow but soon the guards are upon you and, whilst you despatch them with a series of kicks and punches, Akira has sent another arrow straight through your neck and out the other side. It is all over and you die in a pool of blood.

162

260

Carefully you pour out the Flash Powder, just as he looks away, and duck down behind the chest again taking out your flint and tinder. Then you shoot up and strike the flints together. There is a click; the figure turns to you, a spark flies to the Flash Powder and he turns away just as you narrow your eyes and reach for a Shuriken. A bright flash fills the room, and it is as day for a moment. You hurl the Shuriken. Turn to **239**.

261

Too late you realise that it will be very difficult to use this kick as the bodyguard charges shield-first up the stairs, since you cannot possibly kick at the lower part of his body while standing above him. You kick anyway, but he takes it on his shield and his momentum carries him onward – you are knocked back by his shield. Other guards gain the roof of the Keep behind him and you will soon be surrounded. You may sprint across the roof of the Keep and try an enormous leap, hoping to clear the castle wall and land in the moat far below (turn to **34**), take the first opportunity to use the skill of Feigning Death, if you have it (turn to **178**), throw some Flash Powder onto the glowing charcoal brazier if you have any left (turn to **192**) or fight it out (turn to **206**).

262

There is nothing you can do as conscious thought slips from you and you fall into nothingness, your mind completely enslaved. You have no memory now, no thought of your own. You are her servant, and it is you, not the O-Bakemono, that will terrorise the village so effectively now. It is also you who will be forced to give the Scrolls of Kettsuin to the followers of Vile.

263

You recognise the acrid smell of Spiderfish venom but you know your body can overcome its ravages. Even so, a wave of pain and nausea comes over you and you stagger. In that moment, your opponent, with a quick exhalation of triumph, hurls a Shuriken. You desperately try to swing away from it but it nevertheless thuds into your thigh. Lose 3 Endurance. If you are still alive, the nausea passes and you stand erect, plucking the Shuriken from your leg. The other Ninja starts in amazement, and then you can see understanding in his eyes, and hear a muted 'Of course,' spoken under his breath. You use this moment to attack again. Will you try a Forked Lightning Strike kick (turn to 55), a Tiger's Paw chop (turn to 304) or try the Whirlpool throw once more (turn to 87)?

264

The Narwhal bears you through the sea, past shoals of demonfish and still the globe of air around your head allows you to breathe normally. You plunge through a floating wall of giant sea-cucumbers and there is golden sand beneath you. The whale cruises towards an enormous clam in which a handsome blue-skinned Sea-Elf is held fast. The water is creamed, bubbling white, as a host of Sea-Jackals dart towards you, but the Sea-Elf is talking to the Narwhal which races through them and buries its horn in the clam. The Sea-Elf springs free and

grasps your costume, pulling you towards the surface as the Sea-Jackals attack. Will you swim with him (turn to **375**) or break free and try to reach the surface alone (turn to **392**)?

265

The crossbow bolt in the effigy's third hand discharges with a twang and buries itself through your back and into your heart. You fall dying to the marble floor of the temple. Mandrake stands over you and says, 'Honoric will be pleased. He still lives, Ninja, and I have earned five thousand golds. It was nice of you to come to me, although I was looking forward to a stroll in the gardens of the monastery to Kwon this afternoon.' You die at his feet and he will sell the Scrolls of Kettsuin to Honoric, if he really still lives, for two kings' ransoms. You have failed.

266

The magician, whose green cloak bears a symbol of five cloth-of-gold arrows pointing outwards from a central hub, says, 'If you are truly a reverencer of Kwon, the Redeemer, then you will help my friends against the undead spirit of the Barbarian Warlord. You look more like an a-a-assassin to me.' He blinks nervously. Will you do as he bids and enter the cloud of yellow gas (turn to **397**) or attack him in case he is trying to trick you (turn to **290**)?

267

The hatchet-faced adviser asks the Barbarian Overlord if he should use the Chalice of Visions Ulrik nods and you wait nervously, as the sharp-nosed man leaves the hall. Do you have an opal ring from AVENGER!? If you do, turn to **118**. If you do not, turn to **110**.

268

Your foot lashes out and smashes the skull of the first wardog as it leaps for your throat, but you are assailed by the other three all at once. Dodging and kicking you are a blur of motion as you try to defeat the slavering hounds. Another falls beneath your smashing blows but not before his jaws sink into your leg: lose 4 Endurance. If you are still alive you must choose which of the two remaining dogs to aim your next crushing kick at.

	FIRST WARDOG	SECOND WARDOG
Defence against kick:	6	6
Endurance:	14	12
Damage:	1 Die + 1	1 Die + 1

If you win turn to **353**. If the wardogs still live, one of them leaps for your throat while another clamps its jaws on your wrist, if it has not done so already. Your Defence against the first wardog is 8, or 6 if the other now has your arm in its grip. If this is the second or more combat round, then the second already has you in its grip and you lose 2 Endurance as it tries to drag you to the ground. It will not release you until either you or it is dead. If it has not yet grabbed you, your Defence against it is 7. If you survive, continue the battle by returning to the top of this paragraph.

269

With blurring speed you spit a needle at Jikkyu's throat. It flies true but somehow, incredibly, it has

little effect, leaving only a slight gash to mark its passage. In a moment Akira has an arrow ready in his bow and Jikkyu has shouted for the guards. You manage to avoid Akira's first arrow but soon the guards are upon you and, whilst you despatch them with a series of kicks and punches, Akira has sent another arrow straight through your neck and out the other side. It is all over and you die in a pool of blood.

270

You slip quickly past the opening, shielding the flame of your torch behind your body, but your ears tell you that a horde of beings inhabit what must be a large cavern, or so you judge by the resounding echoes. You hurry on down the tunnel. Turn to **252**.

271

You race down the steep steps beyond the door; a guardsman's crossbow bolt whistles over your head but you are lost to sight in a twinkling down the stairs beyond. The stairs wind steeply downward beneath the Keep and the walls drip with moisture. The rattle of links of chains alerts you to be quiet as you come to an underground room lit by the glowing coals of a brazier. A young boy chained to the wall goggles at you but says nothing. You are in the torture chamber of Quench-heart Keep. A ducking stool hangs over a pool of water which stretches to the back wall of the chamber. A man bound on a spiked rack moans feebly as the insomniac torturer turns it another notch, stretching the poor man's burn-scarred limbs to the point of dislocation. The torturer has a large axe in his belt and his broad heavily muscled back runs with sweat in the heat of the brazier. He wears heavy, spiked bracelets of leather and the black hood of an executioner. He whirls to face you as the guards, now pounding down the steep steps behind you, shout a warning. You are trapped between the torturer and the guards.

Will you dive into the pool and swim underwater to the back wall (turn to **153**), attack the torturer (turn to **138**), surrender to the torturer (turn to **124**), or call upon Kwon the Redeemer to be your salvation (turn to **107**)?

272

You wait, poised to strike anything that comes through the door, quiet as a mouse, your spine tingling and your breathing soundless and shallow. There is no sound other than the light tinkle of the courtyard fountain and the chirruping of the crickets. Suddenly there is a tearing sound to your right and a sword rips through the wall, its blade narrowly missing you. There is a brief moment when it seems to shimmer like water, laced with ribbons of black in the moonlight, and then it is gone. Will you jump up and climb onto the roof surrounding the inner courtyard (turn to **334**), open the door and roll into the room beyond (turn to **322**) or drive a Winged Horse kick through the wall, approximately one foot above the hole there (turn to **308**)?

273

The goblins use short, stabbing swords in the mêlée and their steeds try to claw and bite you. You jump high and your Leaping Tiger kick sends the ball of your foot lashing out murderously. You may choose which goblin or giant rat to attack but, remember, these goblins are skilful fighters.

	1st GOBLIN RIDER	2nd GOBLIN RIDER	1st GIANT RAT	2nd GIANT RAT
Endurance:	7	8	9	9
Defence:	7	7	5	5
Damage:	1 die	1 die	1 die	1 die

If you are able to defeat them all, turn to **313**. If three or four are still alive, your Defence against their attacks is 6. If, as you dodge and duck, there are any fewer than this, your Defence is 8. Each has an individual attack and you may only Block one of them. If you survive, you may kick again (return to the top of this paragraph) or punch (turn to **258**).

274

The crossbow in the effigy's third hand discharges with a twang and a magical bolt buries itself in your shoulder. Lose 5 Endurance. If you are still alive you run to the street and, using your superb sense of direction, find your way quickly to the Monastery of Kwon. Turn to **42**.

275

Your fist speeds towards the head of the broad-shouldered Goblin King as the Dancing Sword almost cleaves your own head in two.

	GOBLIN KING	DANCING SWORD
Defence v Cobra Strike:	8	—
Endurance:	10	—
Damage:	1 Die	1 Die + 2

You are hampered by having to defend yourself against the Dancing Sword. If you kill the Goblin King, turn to **253**. If he still survives, your Defence against him is 7 and against the Dancing Sword, 6. You may only Block one attack. If you survive you may punch again (return to the top of this paragraph) or use the Forked Lightning Strike kick (turn to **306**).

276

With an enormous effort of will, the kind of willpower you have only developed after years of hardship and rigorous training, you manage to wrench your eyes away from that awful, green visage of consuming enchantment. As you hear the screech of frustration and hate, you stagger, the mental effort draining you physically for a moment. In that instant, you feel a crawling, hot touch at your leg. Turn to **287**.

277

The guardsman's crossbow bolt whistles over your head and you leap into the door which swings open. Your heel catches a slightly raised flagstone and a trap discharges with a click and double thud behind you, but you are lost to sight in a twinkling down the stairs beyond. They wind steeply downward beneath the Keep and the walls drip with moisture. The rattle of links of chains alerts you to be quiet as you come to an underground room lit by the glowing coals of a brazier. A young boy chained to the wall goggles at you but says nothing. You are in the torture chamber of Quench-heart Keep. A ducking stool hangs over a pool of water which stretches to the back wall of the chamber. A man bound on a spiked rack moans feebly as the insomniac torturer turns it another notch, stretching the poor man's burn-scarred limbs to the point of dislocation. The torturer has a large axe in his belt, and his broad, heavily muscled back runs with sweat in the heat of the brazier. He wears heavy, spiked bracelets of leather and the black hood of an executioner. He whirls to face you as the guards, now pounding down the steep steps behind you, shout a warning. You are trapped between the torturer and the guards.

Will you dive into the pool and swim underwater to the back wall (turn to **153**), attack the torturer (turn to **138**), surrender to the torturer (turn to **124**) or call upon Kwon the Redeemer to be your salvation (turn to **107**)?

278

You turn from Mandrake and the forbidding effigy of the god and run for the doorway. Make a Fate Roll but subtract 2 from your Fate Modifier as you are in the temple to Torremalku the Slayer, where luck may desert you. If Fate remains with you, turn to **274**. If she turns her back on you, turn to **265**.

279

Taking a needle in your hand you punch it through the sandpaper-like skin of the Sea-Jackal as it attacks, but another clamps its jaws on your leg and shakes you like a rag doll. Lose 5 Endurance. If you are still alive, the first Sea-Jackal threshes in agony and you kick out to discourage the others. The Sea-Jackals let you go, and you swim for the shore. Turn to **417**.

280

The monks see what you are doing and your target drops to the floor. Seeing this you whirl and spit your needle at another of them, taking him by surprise. You are already hurdling his falling body as the poison takes hold, and you reach the door before they can grab you. You sprint past the city gates towards an apple orchard and ducking and weaving between the trees in an effort to lose your pursuers you decide to turn to the north and the Goblin's Teeth Mountains, guessing that this is the direction of escape that they would deem most unlikely. As you near the mountains you hear the baying of hounds. Turn to **336**.

281

Even as Cassandra tumbles to the floor Tyutchev is manoeuvring to strike at you. When he does, you parry again and again as the point of his sword stabs at you from left and right, high and low. He feints at your leg then raises the tip of his sword towards your chest. Your Defence as you try to block with your arm guards is 7. If you fail to parry his sword, it pierces your lung; lose 8 Endurance. If you are still alive, as Cassandra rises groggily to her feet, you leap back and are about to begin a series of kicks and punches when the left hand wall of the cellar caves in with a thunderclap, and dust fills the room. Turn to **404**.

282

As you wait, your keen senses pick up something strange about Jikkyu. The outline of his head seems to blur and a hideous demonic visage is superimposed over it for a brief moment. Was it a trick of the poor light or is Jikkyu not what he appears to be, you ask yourself? Then Akira says, 'Let us continue this once we have heard what message the Dai-Bakemono has sent.' With that he looks up at you expectantly, his throat exposed. Will you hurl a Shuriken at Akira's throat (turn to **324**), spit a needle at Akira's throat, if you have that skill (turn to **315**), hurl a Shuriken at Jikkyu (turn to **259**) or spit a needle at Jikkyu, if you have that skill (turn to **269**)?

283

Ulrik Skarsang appears satisfied but the adviser says, 'Should we allow a man with blood on his conscience amongst us, Overlord? He may have fallen into the habit of senseless killing.' He questions you further and you tell him that you have come from the east, but no more. At length, Ulrik tells you that the only ship sailing to the far south from Ulrik's Haven is his personal merchantman, *Sack of the South*, but that she will not return to port for two tendays. He says that you are welcome to free passage south if you care to wait so long and indicates that the interview is over. You leave the hall and bed down for the night in an old manger in an empty cow-shed. Do you have an opal ring from AVENGER!? If you do, turn to **234**. If you do not, turn to **224**.

284

You dodge and spin, flailing towards the slavering jaws of the wardogs with your feet, as they try to tear your throat out.

	FIRST WARDOG	SECOND WARDOG
Defence against kicks:	6	6
Endurance:	14	16
Damage:	1 Die + 1	1 Die + 1

If you win turn to **353**. If the wardogs still live, one of them leaps for your throat while the other clamps its jaws on your wrist if it has not done so already. Your Defence against the first wardog is 8, or 6 if the second now has your arm in its grip. If this is the second or more combat round, the dog already has you in its grip and you lose 2 Endurance as it tries to drag you to the ground; it will not release you until either you or it is dead. If not, your Defence against it is 7. If you survive continue the battle by returning to the top of this paragraph.

285

The Shuriken speeds towards you but time itself seems to slow as, with precise judgement, you pluck the Shuriken out of the air and send it spinning back at your opponent. His eyes widen with astonishment at this but, with a shout, he reaches up with both hands, draws his sword with one incredibly swift motion and knocks the Shuriken aside. There is the clear ring of steel on steel and a whirring hum as the Shuriken twists away, followed by a crisp tearing sound as it goes in and out through the paper-thin wall. There is a pause as you both stare at each other, the insistent flutter of shreds of the torn wall in a sudden night breeze echoing the flurry of explosive violence. He stands, presenting only the side of his body to you, right foot forward, left knee bent and at right angles to his body, sword-hip pointing up at your throat, arms extended. You begin to circle each other warily. Turn to **22**.

286

The opening is at the edge of a huge cavern. A fire burns fifty feet away and, in its light, you make out dozens of dark, bent-limbed beings, chattering and squabbling amongst themselves. They are goblins, but there are too many to guess their number in the darkness of the cavern. You draw back but not before a sharp-eyed little nipper squeals and points at you. Her mother turns to silence her with a slap, but catches sight of your torch as you slip past the opening, and soon there is a hue and cry behind you. Turn to **252**.

287

You look up to see that the Hannya is upon you; great coils as thick as your torso slither around you and you are lifted into the air. She opens her mouth, drawing her lips back over the fanged teeth, hissing, preparing to draw you to her in an embrace of death. The coils burn with the fires of hell and their heat sears your skin. Lose 3 Endurance. If you are still alive, you put the pain from your mind and prepare to attack – luckily, your arms are still free.

Will you spit a needle at her face, if you have that skill (turn to **360**), reach into your costume, daub Cassandra's dagger with the Blood of Nil, if you have both these items, and plunge it into the Hannya (turn to **247**) or use Inner Force, if you have any left, and drive an Iron Fist at the point of her chin (turn to **298**)?

288

As you step aside, the Bailiff's bodyguard trips and your blow sends him flat on his face with a clang of armour meeting stone. He is only stunned but the other guards think you have killed him with a single blow. One of them catches sight of Yaemon's body on the roof and panics. As you advance once more he turns his sword against his fellows and tries to carve his way through them. You follow down the staircase as they retreat to regroup, anxious to avoid the blade of their panicked comrade. You are hot on their heels but the last guard throws himself flat on the floor as you come to the hallway at the bottom of the stone stairs. There is a doorway ahead of you but the other guards have lined up on either side of the hallway, waiting for you. Did you kill the Keep's torturer in the dungeon in Book 1: AVENGER!? If you did turn to **302**. If you did not, or have not played AVENGER!, then turn to **314**.

289

Hardred takes you inside the monastery and you tell him what has happened. It becomes obvious to him that Mandrake, a master of disguise, has been commissioned to murder you. You waste no time in hurrying with an armed escort to the port, where a sleek merchantman, *The Winged Serpent*, rides at anchor. Hardred gives you a parting gift of five Shuriken and says that he will pray for you daily. He tells you that the ship will take you to Lemné on the Island of Plenty, where many worship Eo, the god of peace and well-being. You thank him and thank Kwon, before concealing yourself below deck. Turn to **84**.

290

As you spring towards him he steps backwards in horror, but a yellow star bursts from his ring. Your Defence against it, as it hurtles towards your chest, is 7. If you fail to dodge it, turn to **230**. If you manage to side-step it you leap into the air and his Defence against your flying Winged Horse kick is only 5. If your foot makes contact, turn to **217**. If he manages to step back out of range you try again, (return to the top of this paragraph).

291

You announce bravely that you are a Ninja, an able assassin, and you offer to trade skills. Mandrake's hand moves on the altar and a noise above prompts you to dive to your left in case of a trap. It is to no avail; a huge net descends over the area in which you have been standing, trapping you in its mesh. As you watch helplessly the effigy of the assassin's god, Torremalku the Slayer, comes to life. It leans towards you and the box of curses which it holds in its fourth hand flies open. You are afflicted by every

disease known to man and you are dead within the minute – but not before Mandrake says, 'Honoric will be pleased. He still lives, Ninja, and I have earned five thousand golds. It was nice of you to come to me, although I was looking forward to a stroll in the gardens of the monastery to Kwon this afternoon.'

You die at his feet and he will sell the Scrolls of Kettsuin to Honoric, if he really still lives, for two kings' ransoms. You have failed.

292

The Sea-Jackal threshes in agony and falls to the coral beneath while the others whirl away from you and are soon lost in the green haze of the deep. You swim towards the surface, but a great bulk is looming towards you at great speed. It is a whale with a six-foot slender horn on its forehead. If you would like to try grabbing its horn and then kicking its large eye, turn to **208**. If you would rather wait to see what it will do, turn to **316**.

Eventually, the tunnel opens out into a large cavern with a huge fire in the middle. On the far wall is a crude altar stained with ominous black patches and adorned with black candles and a hideous idol, a few feet in height of a creature half man, half insect. In the corner lies a pile of material – the possessions of the villagers that are of any worth. Just ahead of you is a young girl, the farmer's daughter, chained to a stake near the fire her face streaked with tears and the dirt of the cavern. Nothing else is to be seen. As you step forward, the girl sees you and her eyes stare in surprise and hope. Then she shouts a warning, nodding to your right and you dive into the cavern and roll to your feet. A foul sight greets your eyes. It is an enormous twenty-foot serpent, its coils at least two feet wide, with the torso of a human woman, her eyes green and luminous, her face twisted and evil and framed with long tangled black hair; fanged teeth protrude from her red lips – she is the Hannya, a witch who worships a Demonlord and in return is given the body of a serpent. As you stand in shock for a brief moment, her hands weave in the air and she mumbles arcane words. Her eyes seem to grow larger, more luminous and you cannot look away. They seem to envelop you and you can feel your soul being drawn into the vast expanse of her eyes, a great green nothingness, where you will be forever enslaved to her will. Desperately, you try to retain control of your mind. If you have the ability to Feign Death, and wish to use it, turn to **236**. Otherwise, you are in the lap of Fate:

If Fate smiles on you, turn to **276**.
If Fate turns her back on you, turn to **262**.

294
You reach the tree just as four wardogs rush at you.

They are like black wolves, with viciously spiked collars and claws tipped with steel. Will you kick (turn to **268**) or punch (turn to **243**) as they rush at you?

295

The crossbow bolt catches you in the shoulder, embedding itself inches deep. Lose 5 Endurance. If you are still alive, you try to control your pain as dimly you hear the guard calling for help. Will you try to force an entry through one of the windows (turn to **183**) or continue your climb to the courtyard below (turn to **225**)?

296

You try to twist aside at the last moment but the Shuriken tears into your thigh and a wave of pain washes over you. Lose 3 Endurance. If you are still alive you hear him shout as he reaches up and draws his sword with both hands in one incredibly swift motion. He stands, presenting only the side of his body to you, right foot forward, left knee bent and at right angles to his body, sword-hip pointing up at your throat, arms extended. You begin to encircle each other warily. Turn to **22**.

297

The brigands' leader lies horribly twisted. The others, filled with fear at the sight of what you have done, have run in panic and are soon lost to sight. As you examine the fallen man a rent in the cloth which covers his shield catches your eye. The cloth shows the black raven of the northern Reavers but you strip it away to reveal a silver sword hanging from a silver thread against a background of darkest sable. These men were no brigands. You have killed another captain of the Legion of the Sword of Doom. You search his body but find only one thing of interest, a wax tablet containing his orders: to scour the borderlands between Dwarrowhame, in the lands of the dwarves and Harith-si-the-Crow and to capture or kill any Ninja found there. You pocket the tablet and continue on your way towards the valley of the River Crow. Turn to **21**.

298

With a deep guttural cry, you smash your fist into her face and the power is enormous as the Inner Force leaves you. Her head cracks back and the Hannya's neck snaps like a twig. The eyes stare upward, the head lolling lifelessly. But the coils, demon-spawned, continue to constrict and they still burn with a heat not of this world. Your ribs crack and your costume ignites. Unable to escape, you are burnt alive. At least the Hannya dies with you, and the village will be saved.

299

You dodge to the side and grasp the leather straps on the armour of the first goblin as he rides past you, attempting to use a variation of the Whirlpool throw to hurl him from the saddle. He is surprised by the speed of your action and his Defence is only 4. If you succeed in throwing him you have time to knock him senseless with a deft Tiger's Paw chop. His Defence is 6 and if you hit him he slumps unconscious. Whether you succeed or fail you may now either punch (turn to **258**) or kick (turn to **273**). You may also note that the first goblin is out of the fight.

300

You do not even feel the acid as it appears to splash against you; it was merely an illusion. You strike at Tyutchev but the magical black cloak which he wears makes him appear to be closer than he really is and you miss as he steps back, quick as a cat. As he advances once more, flourishing his sword, the left hand wall of the cellar caves in with a thunderclap and dust fills the room. Turn to **404**.

301

The monster lunges at you with its powerful taloned hands. You decide that it is impossible to throw the many-legged beast. Will you use the Iron Fist punch (turn to **173**), the Leaping Tiger kick (turn to **166**) or, if you have played Book 1: AVENGER! and learnt this kick, Kwon's Flail (turn to **156**)?

302

The door opposite leads down to the castle dungeon, where you killed the Keep's torturer and set the prisoners free earlier this night. Beyond the torture chamber lies a dead beast called an Elder god, and a grille which leads to freedom beyond the garden moat. You remember that there is a crossbow trap which may be primed to go off if you step on a certain flagstone, so you use a flying Winged Horse kick to clear the flagstones and push open the door in one motion. As you leap, one of the soldiers unleashes a bolt from a crossbow. If you have the skill of Arrow Cutting you are able to knock the quarrel aside with your iron-rodded forearm. If you do not have this skill the bolt buries itself in your side and you lose 6 Endurance, but sail through the door and leap down the steep stairs beyond it. The soldiers follow with a clatter of mail as you burst into the torture chamber. The ducking stool still hangs over the pool of water and the dead torturer with his spiked leather bracelets and black hood is still face down in the icy pool. You dive in and swim towards the spot where you hope to find the water-filled tunnel, knowing that the soldiers will not be able to follow. You soon find an opening under the water but to your surprise there are two tunnels; you only saw one when you came this way before, so which is it?

Will you swim down the wider tunnel on the left (turn to 320) or the narrower tunnel on the right (turn to 332)?

303

Your torch spits as you pace silently along the tunnel, the edges of which are chipped and cracked. It must have taken the work of many hammers to mine, but little care has been taken to smooth the walls. After a while your sharp ears catch the hum of chattering voices, and a vague smell of offal reaches you. There is a glow cast on the tunnel wall ahead from what must be a large opening. You inch your way towards it. If you wish to look through the opening, turn to **286**. If you would rather hurry quickly past, turn to **270**.

304

He thrusts at your chest. You act quickly, stepping in and blocking his sword arm with your left arm and then hacking down at the side of his neck with your right hand.

NINJA
Defence against Tiger's Paw chop: 6
Endurance: 19
Damage: 1 Die + 2

If you have reduced him to 0 or less Endurance, turn to **13**. If he still has Endurance, he spins away and then feints at your head before bringing his sword down in a wide arc, hoping to cut you from left shoulder to right hip. Your Defence against this is 7 as you try to cartwheel away. If you survive the attack, will you try a Forked Lightning Strike kick (turn to **55**), a Whirlpool throw (turn to **87**) or another Tiger's Paw chop (return to the top of this paragraph)?

305

The sounds of retching continue as you step forward. The young magician starts in fright at the sight of you in your black Ninja costume and he lets his right hand drop languidly towards you, revealing a sun-bright jewelled ring. Will you leap to the attack (turn to **290**), tell him that you worship Kwon, the Redeemer (turn to **266**), say that you have no quarrel with him (turn to **257**) or order him to give you the ring (turn to **241**)?

306

Your foot strikes twice at the Goblin King's belly and head as the Dancing Sword almost spears your chest.

	GOBLIN KING	DANCING SWORD
Defence against Forked Lightning Strike:	7	—
Endurance:	10	—
Damage:	1 Die	1 Die + 2

You are hampered by having to defend yourself against the Dancing Sword. If you kill the Goblin King, turn to **253**. If he still survives, your Defence against him is 7 and against the Dancing Sword, 6. You may only Block one attack. If you survive you may kick again (return to the top of this paragraph) or use the Cobra Strike punch (turn to **275**).

307

You awake to see, in the moonlight, the shaven-headed figure stooping over you. Before you can move he knocks you senseless with an ebony rod and then, after taking the Scrolls of Kettsuin, slits your throat. He was an assassin sent to kill you by the monks of the Scarlet Mantis and he has stealthily done his work. You have failed.

308

You lift your left leg and smash the side of your foot through the paper-thin walls with an explosive cry. You feel your foot connect and there is an answering cry of surprise and pain, and the sound of a body hitting the floor. With lightning speed you dart forward, wrench the door open and roll into the room and to your feet. The moonlight pools faintly into the room and you can see a figure rising to his feet, some way in front of you. There is a pause as you both stare at each other, the insistent flutter of shreds of the torn wall in a sudden night breeze echoing the flurry of explosive violence. Your assailant is dressed as you are save for the scab-barded curved sword or Ninjato strapped to his back. You may note that he has lost 3 Endurance for your Winged Horse kick. With a shout he reaches up and draws his sword with both hands in one incredibly swift motion. He stands, presenting only the side of his body to you, right foot forward, left knee bent and at right angles to his body, sword-hip pointing up at your throat, arms extended. You begin to circle each other warily. Turn to **22**.

309

You have slain a so-called 'immortal', thus delivering Orb from one of the beasts which roamed the world before man came from the stars. Breathing deeply but silently, you pass by the fallen hulk and up a narrow tunnel, at the end of which is an opening to the sky, blocked by a grille in the ceiling. You brace your back against one wall of the tunnel and with your feet against the other, edge your way up to the ceiling where you lift the grille and throw it aside. You climb out onto the grass beyond the moat. You have escaped from Quench-heart Keep, at least for the moment. As you consider which way to turn you hear the baying of bloodhounds and the yelps of wardogs. Will you skirt the castle and run towards the Goblin's Teeth Mountains that tower above it (turn to 336), run south towards the Sea of the Star (turn to 362), or head for the City of Druath Glennan (turn to 409)?

310

The Moat Horror's suckered grip relaxes and you break free from the folds of rubbery flesh and swim powerfully to the surface, your lungs bursting. You pull yourself out over the grass at the moat's edge and a bullfrog croaks nearby. You have escaped from Quench-heart Keep, at least for the moment. As you lie panting in the darkness, you hear the baying of bloodhounds and the yap of wardogs. They are hunting you! Will you run towards the Goblin's Teeth Mountains that tower before you (turn to 336), run south towards the Sea of the Star (turn to 362) or circle Quench-heart Keep and head for the City of Druath Glennan (turn to 409)?

311

As you step through the harbour gate a party of monks of the Scarlet Mantis close in on you. They are ten strong and they worship Vile, the evil brother of your god Kwon. A message has reached them that Yaemon, Grandmaster of Flame, lies dead by your hand. Each one of them would gladly die to avenge him and they attack fearlessly. If you are a skilled Acrobat and wish to draw them on towards the harbour wall before somersaulting over their heads into the water, turn to **381**. If you have the skill of Poison Needles and wish to use one, turn to **388**. If not, you must give battle – turn to **83**.

312

The King's chief adviser, a thin man with a hatchet-shaped face, says, 'Kneel, dog, to Liege-Chief Ulrik Skarsang, Overlord of this Haven of men!' You decide that you are not going to allow them the pleasure of seeing you kneel so you leap over the heads of the nearest onlookers and quit the great hall before the slow barbarians can move. Ulrik's Haven is soon far behind you as you travel south, and then west across the wild terrain towards Wargrave Abbas. Turn to **131**.

313

As you fell the last of your assailants, the horde of goblins still chasing you is not far behind. You leave your Shuriken, if you used one, and run on again, your lungs on fire from the effort, limbs heavy with fatigue. The tunnel is now lit with crude ornamental lanterns and you run onward until, rounding a corner, you surprise the biggest goblin you have ever seen. He has been counting out gold coins which he shoves under a cloth before picking up a long sword which is clearly not of goblin origin and seems absurdly large for him to wield. He wears a dented copper crown and rusty ring-mail armour. You have still found no way out of the goblin caves but there is another tunnel behind the Goblin King. If you are skilled with Poison Needles you may wish to use one (turn to **339**), or you may hurl a Shuriken

if you have one left (turn to **355**) or you may simply run to the attack (turn to **368**).

314
Your only real choice seems to be the door ahead of you and you move towards it, ducking suddenly as one of the guards fires his crossbow at you. Make a Fate Roll. If Fate smiles on you, turn to **277**. If Fate turns her back on you turn to **255**.

315
You have a needle on your tongue and you shoot it towards Akira in a flash. It pierces his throat and his eyes widen in surprise, and glaze over as the venom takes effect. He slumps to the floor, jerking spasmodically. Jikkyu's face is a mask of astonishment, mixed with a trace of fear as he spits out one word, full of hate and malice, 'Ninja!' Turn to **338**.

316
The Narwhal turns aside at the last moment and you catch sight of a crystal dagger buried in its back, close to its blow-hole. You catch one of its fins and pull yourself onto its back as it hurtles through the sea at amazing speed. You pull out the dagger and it falls to the bottom. The whale swims on, either

happy to tow you or oblivious of your presence. Turn to **264**.

317

You slump to the floor, apparently lifeless, one leg bent unnaturally, and stop breathing. There is silence in the cellar as they watch for any signs of life. After a minute or so, Cassandra bends to place a looking glass before your face. Your breathing is too shallow even to cause condensation and she pronounces you dead. There is a ring of victorious defiance in her voice as she spurns you with her foot before walking away. Suddenly the left hand wall of the cellar caves in with a thunderclap and dust fills the room. You return to consciousness in a twinkling and leap to your feet. Turn to **404**.

318

There is a grinding noise as the stone trap-door above you moves back into place. You light a torch which shows you that you are in a narrow tunnel. You climb up to the trap-door but it is too heavy for you to move. Descending to the tunnel once more you have no choice but to follow its meandering down into the depths beneath the Goblin's Teeth Mountains. Turn to **303**.

319

You step through into near darkness. As your eyes quickly become accustomed to the light you realise that the young man has slipped away but the sight that greets your gaze is breathtaking. What had looked like nothing more than a broken-down warehouse from the street, which you had passed earlier without a second thought, is in fact the temple to the god of assassins, Torremalku the Slayer. There is gold and silver everywhere, the coinage of murder

melted into fair-seeming candelabra and altar ornaments. In the centre of the dark hall is a great effigy of the god himself. It is dressed in a quilted, black leather jerkin and tight black velvet trousers with an executioner's mask. It has four arms, like the Son of Nil, but one holds a dagger dripping white venom; another a purple-jade cup of poison; a third a crossbow with a runewritten bolt and the name 'Everyman' scored upon it in silver; whilst the fourth holds a box of curses. As you study the statue a man dressed in conscious imitation of it approaches and introduces himself as Mandrake. To your surprise he has an open, friendly face and a sandy mop of wayward hair. He stands next to the altar. If you still feel confident enough to trade skill for skill with Mandrake, turn to **291**. If you suddenly feel that you would be better off out of the temple and flee in fear turn to **278**.

320

You swim powerfully along the underground tunnel for a minute, before surfacing in a dark cavern. You remember the smell of putrefying flesh which greets you, and you inch your way along the cavern wall, past the dead body of the Elder god. At last you are below the dead monster's feeding hole and you leap up and grab the metal casement into which the iron grille fits. You haul yourself out onto the grass beside the grille and pause in the darkness to gain your breath – you have escaped Quench-heart Keep, at least for the moment. As you consider which way to turn, you hear the baying of bloodhounds and the yelp of wardogs. Will you skirt the castle and run towards the Goblin's Teeth Mountains that tower above it (turn to **336**), run against the south wind towards the Sea of the Star (turn to **362**), or head for the City of Druath Glennan (turn to **409**)?

As you step forward to punch, the beast lowers its head to charge you, bellowing ferociously. You are meeting the giant immortal head on.

THE ELDER GOD
Defence against Iron Fist: 5
Endurance: 22
Damage: 2 Dice + 2

If you win, turn to **309**. If this creature from the forgotten past still survives, it tries to disembowel you with a flick of its head as it falls briefly onto all fours. Your Defence against this is 7. If you survive, you may use the Winged Horse kick (turn to **333**), the Dragon's Tail throw (turn to **349**) or the Iron Fist again (return to the top of this paragraph).

With lightning speed you dart forward, wrench the door open and throw yourself head first at the floor, somersaulting to your feet. As you come up, you catch a blur of movement out of the corner of your eye. A curved blade is whistling towards you, shining like water as it catches the moonlight from the courtyard. You act instinctively, your left forearm coming up across your face to deflect the sword. Make a Block Roll. Your Defence for the block is 6. If you are successful, turn to **367**. If you fail, turn to **378**.

323

As you make the easy climb over the city wall, at a point where a rotted caravan rests against it, you hear someone whispering somewhere in the shadows. At the top you look round and catch sight of a young woman with a face cleverly made up to look like a cat's. She smiles at you but turns away and walks back into the city, and you let yourself down the twenty feet to the ground below. You are not far from the city when a band of horsemen leave the west gate. You decide to take an unexpected route towards the Goblin's Teeth Mountains. As you skirt through woods, knowing that this will slow the horses, the baying of hounds tells you that the men from the Keep are hunting you. As the hounds close in, you run towards the mountains, hoping that you will be able to climb where they cannot and escape west through the peaks. Turn to **336**.

324

With blurring speed you send a Shuriken spinning towards Akira. It rips into his throat, tearing it open and he keels over backwards, gurgling horribly as blood fountains from his neck; he is dead in a matter of moments. Jikkyu's face is a mask of astonishment mixed with a trace of fear as he spits out one word, full of malice and hate, 'Ninja!' Turn to **338**.

325

You take a needle coated in the poison of the Spiderfish from your costume and bury it into one of the pouting suckers which is questing for your face. Nothing happens at first and the sucker closes over your mouth but then the tentacles seem to become limp and you tear yourself from its grip and swim for the surface, lungs bursting. You pull yourself out onto the grass at the moat's edge and pause for breath. You have escaped from Quench-heart Keep, at least for the moment. As you lie panting in the darkness, you hear the baying of bloodhounds and the yap of wardogs. They are hunting you! Will you run towards the Goblin's Teeth Mountains that tower before you (turn to **336**), run south towards the Sea of the Star (turn to **362**) or circle Quench-heart Keep and head for the City of Druath Glennan (turn to **409**)?

326

You protest your innocence but it makes no difference. Either their information that you killed him is certain or they care so little for life that they take yours for the sake of a moment's amusement. Tyutchev's sword buries itself in your skull, and they will use the knowledge contained in the Scrolls of Kettsuin to wreak havoc and bring chaos to Orb.

327

Your Shuriken tears the throat out of the nearest wardog but the second is upon you. You kick sideways at its slavering jaws as it leaps for your throat.

WARDOG
Defence against Winged Horse: 6
Endurance: 12
Damage: 1 Die + 1

If you win turn to **353**. If the dog still lives, it lunges for your throat again. Your Defence is 8. If you survive you decide to lash out with your feet once more. Return to the top of this paragraph.

328

Did you kill the Keep's torturer in the dungeon in Book 1: AVENGER!? If you did, turn to **357**. If you did not or have not played AVENGER!, turn to **370**.

329

The King's chief adviser, a thin man, with a hatchet-shaped face, says, 'In the name of Liege-Chief Ulrik Skarsang, I command you to identify yourself and to state your business in Ulrik's Haven.' Will you tell them that you are Avenger and that you have travelled north to avenge your father (turn to **283**), or refuse to tell them anything other than that you seek to return to your homeland in the south (turn to **267**)?

330

You plunge into the cloud of yellow gas, before the magician can cast another spell and immediately cough violently as the noisome fumes invade your lungs, but you use your powers of mind over matter to control the nausea that threatens to overwhelm you. A great hunched shadow stalks towards you through the murk. It is the spirit of the Barbarian Lord and you will have to attack it. Will you punch (turn to **86**), kick (turn to **74**) or throw (turn to **53**), the undead Warlord?

331

As you fight for your life, Thaum casts a spell and the two panther-like warriors who face you become blurred apparitions; you can barely make out their swords as they cleave through the air like shadows You cannot stand for long against the two who show such mastery of swordplay when you can hardly see them. Cassandra's sword scores your thigh and the cold bites you again. Lose 4 Endurance. If you are still alive and are a skilled Acrobat, turn to **359**. If you are not a skilled Acrobat, your only other choice is to beg for mercy (turn to **374**) or die, leaving the Scrolls of Kettsuin in the hands of those whose only goal is to bring chaos to the world.

332

You swim powerfully down the narrow tunnel but after a minute your head is still touching the top of the tunnel underwater. You swim on, thankful that you have trained yourself to swim great distances underwater in your youth, until your head at last breaks into the dark night air at the edge of the moat. You gasp a few lungfuls of air and then dive once more lest you are spotted by a guard on the castle walls. With powerful strokes you cut through the icy black water right into what feels like a rotting branch. As you grab it to pull yourself to the bank it bends ominously and you are suddenly enveloped in great folds of suckered flesh. You thrash the water as the monster drags you down, ever deeper. You have been trained in combat underwater but not with gargantuan unseen horrors such as this which now holds you in its sucking grip. Will you punch it (turn to 366), kick it (turn to 347), Feign Death, if you have the skill (turn to 211) or if you are skilled with Poison Needles, embed one in its blubbery flesh (turn to 325)?

333

The beast tries to grab you in a crushing embrace but you somersault towards it, under its grasping hands, and roll to your feet, delivering a Winged Horse kick as you do so.

THE ELDER GOD
Defence against Winged Horse kick: 5
Endurance: 26
Damage: 2 Dice + 2

If you kill the beast, turn to 309. If the beast is still alive it tries to grab you and impale you on its great horn. Your Defence against this is 8 as you try to leap back beyond its long reach.

If you survive you may use the Iron Fist (turn to 321), the Dragon's Tail throw (turn to 349) or kick again (return to the top of this paragraph).

334

You jump up and grab one of the eaves of the roof and pull yourself up. You are almost at the roof when the door to the first room slides open and, as you look down, a figure dressed as you are save for the curved scabbarded sword or Ninjato strapped to his back, leaps and rolls to his feet in the courtyard.

Almost in the same movement his hand flickers in and away from him, and a Shuriken, nearly identical to one of yours, whirrs towards you. Do you have the skill of Arrow Cutting? If you do, turn to **356**. If you don't turn to **346**.

335

He lunges at your stomach. You sweep the blade aside with your forearm and he brings it up and down at your head. At the last moment you manage to whip your left forearm up and across your forehead, the force from the blow almost breaking your arm. But the iron rods in your sleeve hold, as they ring like a hammer hitting an anvil. As he steps back and slashes at your legs with mind-boggling speed, you jump high over the sword's path and land on your feet. You are just in time to twist your right forearm up across your chest and catch the blade before it bites into your neck. Seconds later, you bring it back to the left to take another blow which is aimed at the other side of your neck. The high pitched clang of steel on steel echoes into the night and the sleeves of your costume hang in tatters, fluttering in the breeze from the open doors. The other Ninja steps back and pauses, breathing heavily, left arm extended towards you, fingers spread, his right arm behind his head, the blade of his sword pointed down at your throat: an attack to test your skill. You have a brief moment in which to act.

Will you throw a Shuriken (turn to **385**) or, if you have the skill, spit a Poison Needle at him (turn to **372**)?

336

As you climb into the foothills the note of the hounds' baying changes. They have been set free on your trail. The going is tough as you climb into the mountains, but you know that if you reach a rockface you can climb away from all pursuit, for a while anyway. You are struggling towards a wall of dark rock, illumined in the first rays of a grey dawn, when the ground shifts suddenly beneath your feet and you are tumbled down a tunnel. Turn to **318**.

337

You have still not broken past your attackers and now the three who had closed the path behind you join the fray. These, too, are trained soldiers and you cannot withstand the attacks coming from both sides. You fall to the blade of one of the newcomers and in your last dying moments, you hear him say, 'Honoric would have liked to see this. We have recaptured the Scrolls.'

338

Jikkyu bellows in rage and then a startling transformation takes place. Before your very eyes, he assumes what must be his natural form. Where once stood a man, now stands some demonic beast. It is man-shaped but there any resemblance ends. Its skin is a dull red colour with patches of ochre-coloured warty flesh, its legs are short and powerful, supporting an enormous barrelled torso. The arms are long and heavy, ridged with a powerful alien musculature, ending in three-fingered hands with long curving talons. Its head is squat and wide without a neck; it is split by a great lipless gash that opens to reveal triple rows of razor sharp teeth, glistening wetly. Its breath, fetid and rank, steams from its mouth and nostrils, two flat holes. The eyes are deep pits, glowing redly with malevolent evil. You stand, frozen in horror. In one bound it is upon you, its talons biting into your waist. The thing lifts you into the air as if you were made of paper. You struggle desperately, but its strength is enormous and it pulls you inexorably towards its stinking, snapping maw.

Will you reach into your costume, open the phial containing the Blood of Nil and hurl it into its mouth (turn to **369**) or use Inner Force, if you have any left, and drive an Iron Fist punch in between its eyes (turn to **348**)?

339
The Poison Needle streaks unseen towards the Goblin King but as you blow he is lifting the great sword into the air and the needle hits one of the rings in his sleeve-mail and falls harmlessly to the floor. You run to the attack. Turn to **368**.

340
If you possess either a gleaming Sun-Star ring, or a Crystal that holds a drop of blue water within it, you may use one if you wish.

If you wish to use the Sun-Star ring, turn to **231**.
If you wish to use the Crystal, turn to **221**.

If you will not or cannot use either you will have to rely on your martial arts as the hideous monster bears down on you. Turn to **301**.

341

You decide to use your poisonous pieces of Spiderfish, scattering them on the ground behind you as you go. You sprint on into the rays of the dawn and the sound of the chase lulls as, half-starved, the dogs fight over the scraps of fish. The poison acts quickly but two of the wardogs fight the rest off. There are still two wardogs and ten bloodhounds on your trail. You reach the top of a grassy knoll and turn to meet the rush of the two black wolf-like dogs. They have viciously spiked collars and their claws are tipped with sharpened steel. You have time to throw a Shuriken if you still possess one (turn to **327**). If not, or you do not wish to, you must fight them both (turn to **284**).

342

Faster than thought, your arm knocks the hurtling dagger aside, in a reflex motion practised many thousand times. The man posing as Hardred gapes for a moment, then turns to run. You follow but the gardener with whom you exchanged pleasantries this morning emerges from behind the magnolia tree, blocking your way. On the steps of the temple the real Hardred beckons urgently. You run to him but he says, 'Gently, but yes, good news; a ship sails for Tor on the evening tide. I can vouch for the master.' You look around but the imposter has fled and the gardener is nowhere to be seen. Turn to **289**.

343

You walk on for some time, coming at last, full circle, to the Hydra's Heads Inn. You have been followed for some time but in your present elated mood you believe yourself a hero and a match for anyone. If you decide to risk eating at the inn before leaving the city, turn to **386**. If you would rather dash to the gate and out of the city, turn to **194**.

344

You are helpless in your bonds as the men of Quench-heart Keep fasten red hot rings of iron around your wrists and ankles. They begin to argue over whether to torture you to death, or to leave you to swing in one of the Iron-maidens which hang beyond the gatehouse. Kwon will not aid you again so soon and you decide to commit Seppuku, honourable suicide. Biting your own tongue off you bleed to death, cheating them of their sport.

345

You wait until the young man is some way ahead and then turn down a street of weapon smithies and back out of the unguarded gate. You are soon relaxing once more in the shade of the plane tree in the monastery gardens. Turn to **371**.

346

Desperately you twist in an attempt to avoid the Shuriken but it punctures your thigh. Lose 4 Endurance. If you are still alive, an agonising pain washes over you and you lose your grip on the roof and plummet to the ground. As you hit the ground feet first, your wounded thigh gives way and you find yourself on your back. In an instant your assailant is above you, his sword raised over his head to strike, a look of malevolent triumph in his glittering black eyes. You act instinctively, lashing the ball of your foot up at his chest, in a kind of stationary Leaping Tiger, taking him in the chest. The breath is knocked out of him and he is propelled through the air to crash through the paper-thin walls into the room beyond. Realising you have little time, you spring to your feet and run to the doors hoping to catch him still on his back. With lightning speed you dart forward, wrench the door open and roll into the room and to your feet. The moonlight pools faintly into the room and you can see a figure rising to his feet, some way in front of you. He is up too quickly for you. There is a pause as you both stare at each other, the insistent flutter of shreds of the torn wall in a sudden night breeze echoing the flurry of explosive violence. You may note that he has lost 3 Endurance for your Leaping Tiger kick. With a shout he reaches up and draws his sword with both hands in one incredibly swift motion. He stands, presenting only the side of his body to you, right foot forward, left knee bent and at right angles to his body, sword-hip pointing up at your throat, arms extended. You begin to circle each other warily. Turn to 22.

347

Count the number of times you attack the horror in the moat. You cannot see in the black depths; nor can you feel a soft spot in the suckered hide but you whip your foot in a sharp kick into the folds of rubbery flesh. It is difficult to kick with great force underwater.

MOAT HORROR
Defence against kick: 7
Endurance: 17
Damage: None

If you have killed the Moat Horror, turn to **310**. If you have attacked the horror five times and it still lives, turn to **100**. If not, whether or not you managed to hurt the beast with your last kick, you may now punch it (turn to **366**), kick it again (return to the top of the paragraph), use a Poison Needle, if you have the skill (turn to **325**) or Feign Death, again if you have the skill (turn to **211**).

348

With a shout, as you draw on your Inner Force, your fist crashes into its head with a sound like a clap of thunder. Its head whips back and its skull crumples inward. The creature shudders and staggers back, but still holds you. Then the head comes up, mangled and cracked, oozing a foul yellow ichor. Any other living thing could not survive such destruction yet its eyes stare at you, radiating an evil that is almost tangible, driven by some inhuman life force, demonic, a blasphemous travesty of nature. There is nothing you can do as the jaws snap shut, taking your shoulder off, but mercifully the shock kills you before you can be devoured alive.

349

You slide beneath its feet but cannot move its colossal legs. Instead it collapses on top of you, driving the breath from your body and crushing your ribcage. Next the beast, whose sense of smell is acute, impales you on its horn using its massively powerful arms. You are still twitching feebly as it begins to feed on the entrails which have spilled from your body.

350

The road winds up the mountain, a sheer drop on one side. As evening approaches, you round the corner and sight the palace of Lord Kiyamo. It lies in a shallow valley between two peaks, surrounded by magnificent ornamental gardens and a high stone wall punctuated by tall watchtowers. The main gate is hung with banners, emblazoned with the Mons of Kiyamo, glittering in the sun. You approach the guards at the gate and hand them the ivory token. Without a word, they lead you through the gates, into a large open area. A sorry sight greets your eyes. It is filled with hundreds of tired and dirty warriors, many wounded and some dying. But there is victory in the air, despite their pain and fatigue.

Presently, you are led into a richly furnished Reception Hall where you are asked politely to wait. Your guards bow and leave you. A man in white robes adorned with stylised flowers of deep ultramarine comes into the hall. He has two swords, one long and the other short, tucked into a sash at his waist. He introduces himself as Onikaba, Kiyamo's chief adviser, and tells you he has recently returned from the Island of Tranquil Dreams where he has talked much with the Grandmaster of the Dawn. It seems they know of your success in retrieving the Scrolls of

Kettsuin and they pray to Kwon for your safe return. He leads you into a long chamber of polished wood where Lord Kiyamo sits cross-legged in front of a low table, covered in scrolls and maps. Armed Samurai line the walls. He motions for you to sit beside him and tea is served. He is a man in middle years, his shoulders and arms heavy with muscle from repeated practice with the sword. A white bandage swathes his left shoulder, a recent wound. Then Kiyamo speaks:

'Your fame has come before you, Ninja and Avenger. The followers of Vile, Nemesis and Vasch-Ro are howling for your blood whilst the followers of other gods are laughing up their sleeves. All that is clean and wholesome on Orb is rejoicing. I congratulate you.' He bows before you. You thank him and he continues, 'You are too late to help us here I'm afraid. Luckily we managed to win a great victory without your aid. An evil daimio, Jikkyu, had massed a large army of Ronin, bandits and Bakemono or goblins with which he had conquered most of the south. He had the aid of the priests of Nemesis and the monks of Vile and had planned an invasion of the Island of Tranquil Dreams. Jikkyu tried to force the pass in the mountains but we were ready for him and defeated him in a close-run battle. The south is liberated and the road to Iga is open.

Your Grandmaster has sent a monk, Gorobei, to meet you.'

He signals to his retainers who usher the monk in. You recognise the tall, powerful frame of Gorobei from the Temple of the Rock. He greets you and you embrace each other. 'It is good to see you again, Avenger,' he says, his eyes glistening with unshed tears. 'Long have we prayed for you. We shall travel to Iga tomorrow and take ship homeward.' He smiles happily. Kiyamo says, 'You may rest here as my honoured guest tonight. The guest house has been prepared for you. My Bannerman, Hatemoto Hizen and six Samurai shall be your Honour Guard.' You take your leave of Kiyamo and Gorobei and follow Hizen. Turn to **38**.

351

When, after a short while, all you can hear is the sound of men vomiting and the occasional cry of horror you begin to wonder what is happening. The young magician puts his hand to his mouth and stutters an apology. It seems that the fight is going badly for his friends, lost in the fog. He becomes a picture of indecision as he begins a spell, only to stop and begin another, before laying his hand absent-mindedly on a rusty mace. Will you ask him what is happening (turn to **305**) or run to the aid of his friends (turn to **397**)?

352

The needle strikes the monster but it continues to move towards you, apparently oblivious. It is evidently immune to poisons. You have no option but to rely on your martial arts as it bears down on you. Turn to **301**.

353

With all the wardogs dead, the bloodhounds do not dare to attack you, but their baying as they follow you is answered by others in the direction of the castle. The guards have kept their best trackers on the leash so that they may track you down if necessary. You run towards the sea once more, pausing occasionally to threaten any hound which snaps too close to your heels, and come at last to the sea. You plunge into the breakers and swim towards the rising sun. The baying of the hounds is soon lost in the pounding surf but the swell does not worry you. Turn to **23**.

354

He lunges at your stomach. You sweep the blade aside with your forearm and he brings it up and down at your head. At the last moment you manage to whip your left forearm up and across your forehead, the force from the blow almost breaking your arm, but the iron rods in your sleeve hold as they ring like a hammer hitting an anvil. As he steps back and slashes at your legs with mind-boggling speed, you jump high over the sword's path and land on your feet. You are just in time to twist your right forearm up across your chest, and catch the blade, moments before it bites into your neck. Desperately, you try to bring it back to the left to take another blow but you are a split-second too late, and it slashes down across your left shoulder, almost opening it to the bone. Lose 6 Endurance. If you are still alive, you stifle your cry of pain; only your training enables you to withstand the shock to your system. The high pitched clang of steel on steel echoes into the night and the sleeves of your costume hang in tatters, fluttering in the breeze from the open doors. The other Ninja steps back and pauses, breathing heavily, left arm extended towards you, fingers spread, his right arm behind his head, the blade of his sword pointed down at your throat: an attack to test your skill. His eyes glitter as he smiles beneath his hood. You have a brief moment in which to act.

Will you throw a Shuriken (turn to 385) or, if you have the skill, spit a Poison Needle at him (turn to 372)?

355

You hurl the throwing star in a flash, but the Goblin King has hefted the great sword into the air and it seems to twitch in his hands, deflecting the Shuriken so that it only lodges in his shoulder. You may note that he has lost 2 Endurance as you run to the attack. Turn to 368.

356

You twist, holding on with one arm, freeing your

other. The Shuriken hurtles closer and with precision judgement you pluck it from the air and send it spinning back to your assailant in one fluid movement. You hear him gasp in astonishment at this for you have caught him off balance. He is forced to flip into the air, throwing himself through the paper-thin wall, tearing it open and back into the room he came from. Making a quick decision, you drop lithely to the ground and run for the door, hoping to catch him still off balance. With lightning speed you dart forward, wrench the door open and roll into the room and to your feet. The moonlight pools faintly into the room and you can see a figure rising to his feet, some way in front of you. There is a pause as you both stare at each other; the insistent flutter of shreds of the torn wall in a sudden night breeze echoing the flurry of explosive violence. With a shout he reaches up and draws his sword with both hands in one incredibly swift motion. He stands, presenting only the side of his body to you, right foot forward, left knee bent and at right angles to his body, sword-hip pointing up at your throat, arms extended. You begin to circle each other warily. Turn to **22**.

357

The dead body of the torturer whom you killed still bobs face-down in the pool of water which stretches to the back of the torture chamber. The soldiers curse as they fish him out and when they peel off his black leather executioner's hood they see that his flesh is already pale and bloated. Several of them decide to exact some kind of vengeance and you are kicked brutally time and time again until one of them suggests that you be left alive until a new torturer can be found. Lose 6 Endurance for the awful bruising they have inflicted upon you. You can tell from their faces as they leave you alone in the chamber that each one of them hopes to be picked by the Bailiff as the next torturer. When they are gone you use your skill as an Escapologist to dislocate one arm and, by tensing certain muscles and inching your steel-like fingers between the bonds, struggle free. Beyond the pool is an under-water tunnel which leads to a cavern where lies the body of a beast called an Elder god. This you killed in your infiltration of the castle. But, more importantly, there is a grille there too and this leads to freedom beyond the castle moat. You dive into the chill, dark depths and soon find an opening under the water, but to your surprise there are two tunnels – you only saw one when you came this way before, but which is it? Will you swim down the wider tunnel on the left (turn to **320**) or the narrower tunnel on the right (turn to **332**)?

358

The phial ricochets off the creature's head. Its eyes stare at you, radiating an evil that is almost tangible, driven by some inhuman life force, demonic, a blasphemous travesty of nature. There is nothing you can do as the jaws snap shut, taking your shoulder off, but mercifully the shock kills you before you can be devoured alive.

359

With a great shout that distracts your assailants you leap high into the air and double somersault behind

them. They part and Cassandra moves back towards the oak-panelled door. They are beginning to close in again from different sides; Thaum gathers his wits to cast another spell. Then the left hand wall of the cellar caves in with a thunderclap and dust fills the room. Turn to **404**.

360

You place a needle on your tongue but the hot coils tighten around you and the air is forced from your lungs before you can use it to send the needle on its way. The force is inexorable. A rib cracks, your skin burns and then her unnatural fangs are into your neck, leeching your blood and injecting venom. As if from a distance you can hear the captive girl howl in fear and shattered hope. You die in agony.

361

As you bend down and open the neck of the sack, something leaps from it onto your head. It has claws

which gouge into your neck and is like a purplish air-filled ball. The thing squashes itself against your face as you try to knock it away and you cannot see. You can feel a gristly stalk-like tube, however, which forces itself into your mouth as you open it to shout in pain and shock. As you bite on it, a stream of hot liquid shoots down your throat. If you have Immunity to Poisons, turn to **78**. If you have not, you realise, as your chest contracts in a spasm, that you have been poisoned. You are paralysed and the horrible bag-like thing flattens itself across your face so that you suffocate in agony.

362

You set off, judging the way south by the salt smell of the southerly wind which you battle against with a powerful economic stride that eats up the miles. The cries of the dogs change as they are set free on your trail. The bloodhounds track your scent on the wind but it is the wardogs you fear as the first greyness of dawn creeps towards you. You are in sight of the sea when the barking of the dogs changes – you have been sighted. If you sprint you can reach a gaunt, wind-blasted tree which will cover your back (turn to **294**) or if you wish to stay where you are and try something else, turn to **341**.

363

Make a Shuriken Roll. The Son of Nil's Defence is 6. If you are successful, the Shuriken embeds itself in the monster's face. Remember how much damage you have done and subtract it from the monster's Endurance when you close with it. Turn to **301**.

364

Bung Hole Road climbs steadily away from the Hydra's Heads Inn and the area of the All-Mother hostel into a part of the city where the streets are wider and where many of the houses have gardens full of yellow All-Mother-Splendour and moon lilies. You catch sight of a priest who worships Vile, the evil brother of your own god, Kwon, and turn a corner out of his sight. As you walk along, a white dove lands on your shoulder. It bears a small bead in its beak, which it drops into your palm before flying off. On inspection, you find that the bead is hollow and you pull its halves apart to find a ball of parchment. Unravelling it reveals a cryptic message:

Flee, flee as fast as you can.
Flee the city in the direction least expected –
You are being watched.

You swallow the parchment and look around. There is no-one in sight. Will you walk on through the city (turn to **343**), run to the northern wall of the city and climb out over it (turn to **323**) or to the harbour gate to see if you can stow away on a ship (turn to **311**)?

365

The young man does not look back once. He leads you by devious ways through the streets of the city; a person with a less well developed sense of direction would have been utterly confused. At last you stand before what looks like the back of an old grain warehouse. The young man beckons you through a low wooden doorway. Determined to follow your quest for new skills through, you stoop and step through. Turn to **319**.

366

Count the number of times you attack the horror in

the moat. You cannot see anything, nor feel a parti-
cularly vulnerable spot, but you drive your fist in a
short punch whose force is not much lessened by
the icy water.

MOAT HORROR
Defence against Iron Fist punch: 6
Endurance: 17
Damage: None

If you have killed the Moat Horror, turn to **310**. If
you have attacked the horror five times and it still
lives, turn to **100**. Whether or not you managed to
hurt the beast with your last blow, you may now
kick it (turn to **347**), punch it (return to the top of this
paragraph), use a Poison Needle, if you have the
skill (turn to **325**) or Feign Death, again if you have
the skill (turn to **211**).

367

The curved blade rings on the iron rods sewn into
your sleeve, a single clear note, but you turn it aside
as you rise completely to your feet and spin away
from it. You come to rest facing your opponent. The
moonlight pools faintly into the room and you can
see a figure rising to his feet, some way in front of
you. There is a pause as you both stare at each other,
the insistent flutter of shreds of the torn wall in a
sudden night breeze echoing the flurry of explosive
violence. Your assailant is dressed as you are save
for the curved sword or Ninjato grasped in his
hand. He stands, presenting only the side of his

body to you, right foot forward, left knee bent and at right angles to his body, sword-hip pointing up at your throat, arms extended. You begin to circle each other warily. Turn to **22**.

368

As you prepare to flatten the Goblin King, the long sword which he was struggling to heft soars from his hands into the air and begins to fight you on its own. You dodge nimbly but it is as if the sword is wielded by a champion at arms whom you cannot see, or kill. The blade cuts your head: lose 2 Endurance. If you are still alive you must decide what to do. Will you try to snap the Dancing Sword with an Iron Fist punch (turn to **379**), flee the way you came (turn to **394**), or risk everything in an attack on the Goblin King (turn to **407**)?

369

You draw your arm back and hurl the container at the demonic gaping maw. Treat that attack as a Shuriken Roll. Its Defence is 4, as it divines your purpose and tries to close its enormous jaws. If you fail, turn to **358**. If you succeed, turn to **376**.

370

A young boy chained to the wall goggles wide-eyed at you, as the torturer leaves the spiked rack on which he had been stretching the burn-scarred limbs of a poor prisoner to the point of dislocation. A ducking stool hangs over a pool of water which stretches to the back wall of the chamber. The insomniac torturer has a large axe in his belt and his powerful upper torso runs with sweat in the heat of a charcoal brazier. He wears heavy, spiked bracelets of leather and the black hood of an executioner. You cannot see his expression as he examines your bonds and pronounces that he is satisfied with the handywork of the guards. When they have told him that you have killed Yaemon, Honoric and Manse the Deathmage his voice fills with false anger. 'I can see my ingenuity will be stretched to the limit thinking up fitting punishments for you, Ninja.' He orders the guards from the chamber and turns to examine the manacles in a small furnace.

Using your skill as an Escapologist you dislocate one arm and, by tensing certain muscles and inching your steel-like fingers between the bonds, you struggle free. Mercifully, the boy remains silent as you creep like a stalking tiger towards the broad sweating back of the torturer. With a cry you explode into a kick which sends his head flying into the furnace. The boy cheers weakly as you close the furnace door on the neck of the sadistic torturer, muffling his death agonies. You free the prisoners and the boy tells you that there is a way of escape through the underground river which connects the pool in this chamber to the moat. Knowing that you must restore the Scrolls of Kettsuin to safety, you thank him and dive in. Turn to **153**.

371

As you sit cross-legged, musing on the ways of the world, you catch sight of the bald head of one of the monks. He rounds a large magnolia tree and walks towards you, smiling a greeting. It is Hardred, the Grandmaster of the temple to Kwon. 'A ship?' you ask hopefully. Hardred nods his head and reaches inside his brown habit. Something about him seems different today, perhaps his carriage, or the way he has tied the knot at the front of his habit. Will you risk upsetting him, reacting as if he were an assassin (turn to 382) or reflect that your thoughts of Torremalku the Slayer have made you nervous and merely stay alert (turn to 69)?

372

With a deft motion, you place a needle on your tongue and spit hard. The needle slaps into the palm of his outstretched hand. He starts back completely surprised at what you have done – it seems the Ninja of the Way of the Scorpion knows nothing of using Poison Needles in this way. However, he takes it from his hand and casts it aside, saying contemptuously, 'Spiderfish venom! Do you think that I have not spent many years learning to withstand its effect?' Wasting no time in speech, you take the chance to spring forward and attack. Will you try the Forked Lightning Strike kick (turn to 55), the Tiger's Paw chop (turn to 304) or the Whirlpool throw (turn to 87)?

373

The huge monster lumbers towards you and you can see that it resembles a great, hairless ape. It is chained at the ankle with massive iron links, so that it can only reach the entrance to the cavern. The great areas of hanging skin reveal enormous black muscles taut with power. Will you use the Winged Horse kick (turn to 333), the Iron Fist (turn to 321) or the Dragon's Tail throw (turn to 349)?

374

You beg for your life on bended knee. Tyutchev's lips curl in a snarl of disdain; there is a look of disappointment in Cassandra's eyes. If you protest that you did not slay Olvar the Chaos-Bringer, turn to **326**. If you tell them of the great mission you have undertaken from Quench-heart Keep and its importance, turn to **384**.

375

The Narwhal defends you both, fighting viciously, and the Sea-Elf tows you to the surface, swimming far more strongly than you could alone. At last the Narwhal turns for the true deeps of the open sea and the Sea-Jackals give chase. As you break the surface you are surrounded by Sea-Elves and mermen who seem to you to have appeared from nowhere. The elves cluster around you. Their voices ring clear like bells as they thank you for saving their prince. Will you accept their thanks gracefully (turn to **403**) or protest that it was the whale who saved their prince (turn to **411**)?

376

The phial of Blood of Nil hurtles into its mouth just as the jaws snap shut. The creature arches its back and spreads its arms wide, dropping you. It staggers back, shuddering horribly and roaring uncontrollably. It spins around, flailing the air, and crashes to the ground, writhing. It begins to smoke. Huge boils pustulate on its body and burst, spurting plumes of yellow stinking ichor and noxious gasses as it dies. The guards rush in and stop short, transfixed with horror. At that moment, you dart out of the tent and are lost in the night, your mission complete. But it will leave forever a chill of horror engraved on your heart.

A day later it is evening, and you are safe in the polished wooden hall of Kiyamo's Palace. Kiyamo is there with Onikaba and Gorobei. You tell them the events of your mission and they listen with amazement. When you have finished, Kiyamo says, 'Jikkyu was an Arabaru-kami! A demon from hell, able to assume the form of a man. That would explain his power over bandits and Bakemono. No wonder the priests of Nemesis and the monks of Vile were prepared to aid him! I will always be in your debt, Ninja. Already his army has broken up, and my men are scattering them to the five winds even now. The land is free again and the road to Iga open. Rest as my honoured guest here tonight, Ninja. Tomorrow, you and Gorobei can travel south to Iga and take ship to the Island of Tranquil Dreams.' Gorobei turns to you and bows, 'Here, take the Scrolls, for you have carried them always in the face of death and it is your honour to return them to the Temple of the Rock at our home.' You thank him and Kiyamo says, 'My Bannerman, Hatemoto Hizen and six Samurai shall be your Honour Guard. The guest house in the palace gardens has been prepared for you. May the Blessing of Eo go with you!' Turn to **38**.

228

377

The Sea-Elves have brought you beyond the reach of the men of Quench-heart Keep and you decide to spend the day and night recuperating after your ordeal. When you rise early next morning, the sun's warmth and the salty air are invigorating. Your rest has done you good. You may restore up to 4 points of lost Endurance. You are still thousands of miles from home but you feel well able to make the long return journey. You follow the River Flatwater upstream for some while before heading west, skirting a wooded range of tall mountains. The only beings of any interest that you espy are a few stocky mountain dwarves like small specks on a far away hill-top. After two days' travel you leave the woodlands behind and climb towards a line of conical hills. Turn to **415**.

378

The blade rings on the iron rods sewn into your sleeves, but as it does so your unknown attacker twists it aside and down, to slice across your left side as you rise to your feet. Lose 5 Endurance. If you are still alive, you spin away from the curved blade and come to rest facing your opponent. The moonlight pools faintly into the room and you can see a figure rising to his feet, some way in front of you. There is a pause as you both stare at each other, the insistent flutter of shreds of the torn wall in a sudden night breeze echoing the flurry of explosive violence. Your assailant is dressed as you are save for the curved sword or Ninjato grasped in his hand. He stands, presenting only the side of his body to you, right foot forward, left knee bent and at right angles to his body, sword-hip pointing up at your throat, arms extended. You begin to circle each other warily. Turn to **22**.

379

You manage to slam your stone-hard fist into the hilt of the Dancing Sword, but it is made of tempered steel and it merely spins away through the air before returning to slice into your arm. Lose 3 more Endurance. If you are still alive, will you turn and flee the way you came (turn to **394**) or risk everything in an attack on the Goblin King (turn to **407**)?

380

You walk from the peace of the gardens through the unguarded gate into Wargrave itself. You pass a barracks on your left and a tavern called the *Sword-arm's Rest* on your right. You stop an old washerwoman in the street and ask the way to the assassin's guild. She blenches white with fear and runs from you. You ask a soldier but he pretends not to hear. It is the same wherever you go until you begin to feel you will never find your way to Mandrake. At last a young man drops a pebble in the street, near your foot. You stoop and pick it up – two words are scrawled in charcoal on it: 'Follow me'. Will you follow the young man who is dressed in rough woollen homespun jacket and baggy trousers (turn to **365**) or give up on your quest for new skills and return to the monastery gardens (turn to **345**)?

381

You give ground as the monks fan out to encircle you but you reach the edge of the harbour before you are surrounded. You wait for one of them to lunge at you before somersaulting over his head and into the harbour. You can swim more powerfully than they and you cut across the bows of a small jib-sailed fishing boat, surging powerfully out of the water to grab the bowsprit as the bows bear down on you. The boat carries you out to sea before the monks can stop it but it turns west and sails within easy sight of the shore. From your position, hanging below the bows, you can see the monks on the beach – they are keeping pace with the boat. You climb round to the offshore side of the craft, still hanging, this time from the rail, and after a time dive unseen into the depths, hoping to give your pursuers the slip. Turn to **23**.

382

What will you do as the smiling Hardred approaches:

Use a Poison Needle, if you have that skill (turn to **175**)?

Call upon Kwon the Redeemer, if you have not done so already (turn to **150**)?

If you are a skilled Acrobat, you may wish to leap upwards and grab an overhanging branch to pull yourself into the tree (turn to **120**)?

You could hurl a Shuriken at his leg, if you have one (turn to **61**)?

Or simply roll to one side and stand up (turn to **45**)?

383

Your prodigious leap carries you just over the battlements of the castle wall and you dive into the dark depths of the moat with a splash. You are carried deep by the speed of your fall, but it is easy for you to swim across the moat underwater, to avoid any arrows which may be fired from the castle. With powerful strokes you cut through the icy, black water right into what feels like a rotting branch. As you grab it to pull yourself to the bank it bends ominously and you are suddenly enveloped in great folds of suckered flesh. You thrash the water as the monster drags you down, ever deeper. You have been trained in combat underwater but not with gargantuan unseen horrors such as that which now holds you in its sucking grip. Will you punch it (turn to **366**), kick it (turn to **347**), Feign Death, if you have the skill (turn to **211**) or if you are skilled with Poison Needles, embed one in its blubbery flesh (turn to **325**)?

384

Your tale is lengthy and, fortunately for you, interesting. They listen agog until suddenly the left hand wall of the cellar caves in with a thunderclap and dust fills the room. Turn to **404**.

385

You send a Shuriken hurtling towards him but he pulls his sword-arm across and there is a ringing sound as he deflects it with his forearm; he too has Iron Sleeves. As your eyes follow his block, you fail to notice that he is reaching into his costume with his other hand and throwing something at you in return. It appears to be an egg and you have no time to dodge. Do you have the skill of Arrow Cutting? If you do, turn to **416**. If you do not, turn to **405**.

386

In the inn you sit down to a most appetising meal

but later, as you rise to pay, two monks of the order of the Scarlet Mantis vault the bar and five others enter by the main door behind you. They worship Vile, the evil brother of your god Kwon, and a message has reached them that Yaemon, Grandmaster of Flame, lies dead by your hand. Each one of them would gladly die to avenge him and they attack fearlessly. If you are a skilled Acrobat and wish to somersault over their heads to escape, turn to **400**. If you have the skill of Poison Needles and wish to use one, turn to **280**. If not, you must give battle. Turn to **158**.

387

Calmly, you approach the two guards and salute. They nod at you. You say you have an important message for Lord Jikkyu. One of them asks you who it is from. Will you say it is from the chief of the Bakemono (turn to **229**) or that it is from Jikkyu's chief lieutenant, Akira (turn to **242**)?

388

The monks surround you and, noticing what you are doing, your target ducks to the floor. Seeing this, you whirl and spit a needle at another of them, taking him by surprise. You are already hurdling his

falling body as the poison takes hold, and you dive
into the harbour before the others can grab you. You
can swim more powerfully than they and you cut
across the bows of a small jib-sailed fishing boat,
surging powerfully out of the water to grab the
bowsprit as the bows bear down on you. The boat
carries you out to sea before the monks can stop it
but it turns west and sails within easy sight of the
shore. From your position, hanging below the
bows, you can see the monks on the beach – they
are keeping pace with the boat. You climb round to
the offshore side of the craft, still hanging, this time
from the rail and after a time dive unseen into the
depths, hoping to give your pursuers the slip. Turn
to **23**.

389

The hideous Spawn of Nil moves ponderously towards you, its withered tail swaying sinuously from
side to side above its face. Drops of black poison are
collecting on the end of the barbed sting. If you wish
to use your martial arts against the monster, turn to
251. If you would prefer to use any item you may
have picked up on your travels turn to **340**.

390

The Hannya gives a howl of rage at the death of her
servant which echoes around the cavern. Her hands
weave in the air and she mumbles arcane words.
Her eyes seem to grow larger, more luminous and
you cannot look away. They seem to envelop you
and you can feel your soul being drawn into the vast
expanse of her eyes, a great green nothingness,
where you will be forever enslaved to her will.
Desperately, you try to retain control of your mind.
If you have the ability to Feign Death, and wish to

use it, turn to **236**. Otherwise, you are in the lap of
Fate:

If Fate smiles on you, turn to **276**.
If Fate turns her back on you, turn to **262**.

391

The dark cloak which Tyutchev wears makes him
appear nearer than he really is and your needle flies
harmlessly into its folds. There is a sharp pain in
your back; Cassandra has thrown her knife into
you. Lose 3 Endurance. If you are still alive, you
turn and leap to attack her. Turn to **121**.

392

The Narwhal fights viciously but you cannot swim
half as fast as the Sea-Elf, and four Sea-Jackals close
in on you from all sides. All you can do is attempt a
Cobra Strike – turn to **245**.

393

Resting in the shade of a plane tree, you muse on the
quirk of fate that left you an orphan to be brought up
to the worship of Kwon. You have never known any
other god, yet there are many on Orb. You despise
the assassins who worship Torremalku because
they kill for money, not to rid the world of evil. Yet
you have killed many times without a qualm just as

they would kill you if they were paid to. If you would like to leave your poison in the monastery and visit the temple to Torremalku the Slayer, to talk to Mandrake, the Guildmaster of Assassins (you may be able to learn new skills), turn to **380**. If you prefer to relax in the quiet of the gardens, turn to **371**.

394

As you turn and run, the sword, which flies through the air much faster than even you can run, buries itself deep in your back. You fall to the rock floor dead, leaving the Goblin King to puzzle over what strange magicks may be contained in the Scrolls of Kettsuin.

395

As you enter the streets of Harith-si-the-Crow once more, you cast your gaze back to the brooding temple, with its unfathomable frescoes of strange monsters made of beaten copper, greened by the rains of centuries. You hurry quickly from the city of Harith before the servants of Nil realise that you have killed the son of their god, pausing only to stop an Illustran priestess, to ask of the nearest ports on the shores of the Endless Sea. She tells you that one of the nearest ports is Ulrik's Haven on the Great Valley Reaches which pour their cold waters out into that sea. It lies north-west of Harith, but she warns you that it is peopled by buccaneers and barbarian coastal raiders. To the west lies the city of Wargrave Abbas, on the shores of the Endless Sea itself, which she tells you is a wealthy trading port but also a place where there are many training schools for mercenary soldiers. You thank her and leave the city while the gate-guard is chastising an old woman who has spilt her basket of eggs in the street. If you wish to strike north-west for Ulrik's Haven, turn to **135**. If you prefer to continue west towards Wargrave Abbas, turn to **131**.

396

The hideous Spawn of Nil moves ponderously towards you, its withered tail jerking forward occasionally, throwing black gobbets of poison that hiss and steam when they hit the floor. Its mouth yawns wide and the tendrils writhe. If you have a Shuriken and would like to use it, turn to **363**. If you are skilled with Poison Needles and wish to use one, turn to **352**. If you would prefer to use any item you may have picked up on your travels turn to **340**. If you wish to use your martial arts against the monster, turn to **301**.

397

You can dimly see hunched figures in the fog of swirling gas. You leap in, and immediately cough violently as the poisonous fumes invade your lungs, but you use your power of mind over matter to control the nausea that threatens to overwhelm you. You can dimly make out the man in white robes; he is almost helpless, the spiked chains of his flail stirring the gas ineffectually. Beyond him the spirit of the Barbarian Lord, seemingly untroubled by the vapours, is about to attack with a sword that glows vividly in the fog. You pull the priest behind you and prepare to give battle. Will you punch (turn to **86**), kick (turn to **74**) or throw (turn to **53**) the Warlord?

398

You steal into the cavern as the O-Bakemono rises to its feet. Suddenly you dash out from the shadows and, as the scaly beast whirls, you spin to the right on your left foot and whip the heel of your right foot, like a ball and chain, around and into the temple of the O-Bakemono with a shout as you draw on Inner Force. It drops like a rock, its skull crushed and its brain pulped. You turn to face the Hannya as it writhes towards you in surprise. The young girl screams with wild hope. Turn to **390**.

399

Thaum slaps his hand to his cheek in horror. The needle has pierced his skin and the venom courses through his veins setting him on fire. He collapses to the floor and twitches horribly. Your natural cunning, cleverly attacking the magician before he could cast a spell, will stand you in good stead if you live. You may add one to the Attack Modifier of your choice. Tyutchev kneels at his side and tips a potion of some kind down his throat and he begins to recover. There is a sharp pain in your back; Cassandra has thrown her knife into you. Lose 3 Endurance. If you are still alive you turn to meet her attack as she tries to spit you on her sword. Turn to **121**.

400

You wait, in fighting stance, until one lunges at you, before launching yourself in a high double somersault over his head. You land running and are out of the door before they can grab you. You sprint past

the city gates towards an apple orchard and ducking and weaving between the trees in an effort to lose your pursuers, you decide to turn to the north and the Goblin's Teeth Mountains, guessing that this is the direction of escape that they would deem most unlikely. As you approach the mountains you hear the baying of hounds. Turn to **336**.

401

Your prodigious leap does not carry you far enough and you land on the battlements of the castle walls, your body flattened unnaturally by the impact. Death takes you before the pain registers.

402

The farmer gives you directions as to where he thinks the cave might be. As you leave his house you are met by a crowd of expectant villagers who thank you over and over again as you push your way between them. Soon you have reached the wooded foothills of the mountains and it is not long before you have found the tracks of a large, heavy, two-footed creature, its toes obviously clawed – probably the O-Bakemono. You follow the tracks through the tall trees for a half hour or so, when a heavy thumping sound comes to your ears, from the direction in which the tracks are leading. Cautiously you creep forward until you can see where the woods end. You crouch behind a bush and look out from the trees into a clearing in front of a sheer rock-face that climbs up the mountainside. A large and heavy creature is breaking up wood with its bare hands, smashing logs in two. It wears dirty leggings and a filthy tunic over which hang a hotch-potch of metal plates serving as armour. A huge carved wooden club, strengthened with iron bands, lies at its side. Its hands and bare feet are taloned and it looks similar to an ogre of the Manmarch save that its skin is scaly, like that of a fish. It also reeks, a clogging, cloying stench of decay. This must be the O-Bakemono.

Will you quietly steal up, leap onto its back and wrap your Garotte around its throat (turn to **40**), wait and see what happens (turn to **29**), or if you are skilled with Poison Needles, creep up behind it and spit a needle into its neck (turn to **414**)?

403

They offer to escort you to the shore, as your limbs ache from the exertion of staying afloat. As they do, you hear one of the mermen apologising to the elf prince for his brother's mistaken attack on his friend the Narwhal. They are soon lost in the breakers behind you and you are at a silver sandy shore. Turn to **417**.

404

Something slithers heavily into the dust-filled room, out of a dark crypt under the church of Nil. It seems to be ten feet tall but much longer. As it approaches, you make out a hideous human face, with a gaping hole surrounded by feeding tendrils for a mouth. It has four arms and the body of a gigantic bloated centipede. A wicked scorpion's tail dangles a vicious poison barb just behind the awful head. Tyutchev cries out, 'Spawn of the Void, it is Mardolh, the Son of Nil.' As you stand, transfixed by horror, the unnatural fiend moves towards Thaum. He casts a spell and a ball of flame leaves his

hand, erupting into a fireball which withers the
scorpion tail of the Son of Nil. It bellows so loudly
that you are temporarily deafened. Cassandra
scrabbles at the bolt of the oaken door and Tyutchev
and Thaum retreat to the far wall. Tyutchev throws
the Scrolls of Kettsuin to the floor, hoping the
creature will stop for them. Cassandra tears the
door open, runs through and shuts it behind her. A
part of the wall revolves before Tyutchev and he
steps through into a tunnel beyond. Thaum turns at
the last and you see that he has completely changed;
he has polymorphed himself into the exact likeness
of a priest of Nil, Mouth of the Void. He wears a
black cloak mottled with brown like a python, and
the hood looks like a python's head. He points at
you and says, 'Kill this desecrator, O Great One.
This assassin has sworn to return our great god to
the Void.' With this he vanishes and the wall grinds
back into place. You rush to the oak-panelled door
but Cassandra has jammed it shut with something.
You must face a Son of Nil alone. Turn to **396**.

405

Before you can move, the egg explodes in your face
and your eyes are filled with pepper and other
unknown substances. You are completely blinded,
your eyes burning like fire. Desperately, you give

ground, flailing the air with your forearm, hoping to catch his sword. You feel an intense pain just above the knee as your leg is cut from under you. You begin to say something when your head is struck from your shoulders and you die in a fountain of blood.

406

You are given a bunk of your own to sleep on during the long voyage and the captain and crew are civil if distant. The *Sack of the South* is escorted by three galleys of the type used by the northern barbarians for coastal raids. The barbarians do not use slaves as rowers; they row from the open deck, shaded from the sun by their shields which line the ship's rail The weather is good and you sail west, away from the fjords of the Great Valley Reaches, then south, past Wargrave Abbas. As you sail past the city of Doomover you espy five flags on the horizon. Five rakish war-galleys begin to overhaul you. They fly the flag of the League of the Barbican, the war fleet of Doomover, and you know that they are manned by soldiers of the Legion of the Sword of Doom, worshippers of Vasch-Ro the wargod. They were once commanded by Honoric, whom you slew in Quench-heart Keep. The three barbarian galleys turn away to the open sea, mysteriously leaving the *Sack of the South* to her fate. Too late, you realise you are sailing into a trap. The captain orders the sails to be furled and the Barbican ships pull alongside. The barbarians have delivered you into the hands of your enemies. You quickly throw the Scrolls of Kettsuin into the sea, but you are surrounded by enemies, far from land, your plight hopeless. You do the only honourable thing – commit Seppuku – grabbing a buccaneer's sword and plunging it into your own heart. At least the scrolls did not fall into the hands of the Doom Legion.

407

The Goblin King has drawn a short sword with which he defends himself against your sudden onslaught. You will have to parry the attacks of the Dancing Sword with your iron sleeve-rods while trying to kill the Goblin King. Will you use the Cobra Strike punch (turn to **275**), the Lightning Strike kick (turn to **306**), or the Teeth of the Tiger throw (turn to **419**)?

408

You spend two very pleasant days in the gardens of the monastery where the children of the city dwellers come to play. You talk to the monks and learn of the city of Wargrave Abbas. It has a strong mercenary tradition; young men and women come from lands far away to learn the skills of swordplay, taught by the worshippers of Dama, Shieldmaiden of the gods. Dama stands opposite the evil wargod, Vasch-Ro, in the Garden of the gods, and it was she whom Honoric, the Captain of the Legion of the Sword of Doom, sought to imprison in Inferno when he undertook his journey towards the Pillars of Change with Yaemon, Grandmaster of Flame. Wargrave is also a thriving trading port, exporting grain and wool to southern lands. One thing only strikes a sour note – the assassins who revere Torremalku the Slayer have long had a guild where anyone may go to put a price on the head of an innocent man. The worshippers of Torremalku, 'Swift-sure bringer of death to beggar and king', care nothing for life or for death, only for the artistry with which they kill. They pride themselves that few who are brought to their attention live for long, if the price is right. It is their law that none save members of their guild may use poison for any purpose. Turn to 393.

409

You cover the many miles to Druath Glennan in a few hours, arriving soon after the peasants have begun their day's work, harvesting in the fields. Just inside the city gates, nestling among the wooden houses with their brightly painted balconies, is the Hydra's Heads Inn. If you would like to go in and order breakfast after the rigours of your night raid on Quench-heart Keep, turn to 386. If you would rather continue along Bung Hole Road towards the quarters of the well-to-do, turn to 364.

410

With a shout, he reaches up with both hands, draws his sword with one incredibly swift motion and attempts to deflect the Shuriken, but his judgement is slightly off. There is the clear ring of steel on steel, a savage rip as the Shuriken flies on, parting his costume at the shoulder, a whirring hum as it twists away, followed by a crisp tearing sound as it goes on and out through the paper-thin wall. You can see blood, black and glistening, in the pool of faint moonlight, as it trickles from his shoulder. There is a pause as you both stare at each other, the insistent flutter of shreds of the torn wall in a sudden night breeze echoing the flurry of explosive violence. He stands, presenting only the side of his body to you, right foot forward, left knee bent and at right angles to his body, sword-hip pointing up at your throat, arms extended. You begin to circle each other warily. You may note that he has lost 3 Endurance from your Shuriken. Turn to **22**.

411

The prince's voice reminds you of a bard's harp as he praises you for your honesty, saying that you are unlike the landwalkers that he has heard of in stories, for three reasons: 'You are honest, you are not afraid and you are almost a good swimmer.' One of the mermen apologises for the behaviour of his brother who, it seems, mistakenly attacked the prince's friend, the Narwhal. The prince tells the assembled throng that your action in pulling out the crystal knife which goaded it meant that his friend returned to save him. You are fêted by the elves who say they will bear you swiftly to any part of the Sea of the Star that you choose. You decide to return to the Island of Tranquil Dreams from one of the northern sea ports and ask to be taken to the north-west corner of the sea so that you may strike for the coast of the Endless Sea without returning to the Manmarch, where you now have many foes. They pull you effortlessly through the water, their webbed feet beating powerfully until you stand on the shore at the mouth of the river they call Flatwater. They lose some of their grace as they stand out of the water, but you see for the first time how powerful their bodies are.

The prince gives you a crystal shaped like a diamond, with water that stays the blue of the sea inside it, even though there is but a drop. He tells you that smashing it will release an elemental from the plane of seas whenever you are sorely in need of help. You are spellbound by its sparkling beauty as the Sea-Elves dive once more below the waves. Turn to **377**.

412

The gleaming Sun-Star ring explodes in your face; lose 4 Endurance. The magician must have told you the wrong magical word of command. But, if you are still alive, you see that a Sun Star has erupted from the ring as you intended and Cassandra has been hurled back against the oak-panelled door which she bolted behind you. She now lies crumpled at its foot, shaking her head. Thaum finishes his spell and, producing a brass horn inlaid with mother of pearl from within his voluminous robes, pours a river of steaming acid towards you, as Tyutchev leaps aside. The acid sprays towards you, like a geyser. Will you roll to the ground, hoping it will pass above you (turn to **202**) or let it hit you and attack regardless (turn to **300**)?

413

Something slithers heavily into the dust-filled room, out of a dark crypt under the church of Nil. It seems to be ten feet tall but much longer. As it approaches you make out a hideous human face with a gaping hole for a mouth surrounded by feeding tendrils. It has four arms and the body of a gigantic bloated centipede. A wicked scorpion's tail dangles a vicious poison barb just behind the awful head. Tyutchev cries out, 'Spawn of the Void, it is Mardolh, the Son of Nil.' As you stand, transfixed by horror, the unnatural fiend moves towards Tyutchev. It is bellowing so loudly that you are temporarily deafened. Cassandra scrabbles at the bolt of the oaken door, wrenching it open, then slamming it shut behind her. Tyutchev throws the Scrolls of Kettsuin to the floor, hoping the creature will stop for them, and then runs to the far wall where a section of rock revolves and he steps through into a tunnel beyond. The wall revolves once more, grinding shut, so you rush to the oak-panelled door but Cassandra has jammed it shut with something. You must face a Son of Nil alone. Turn to **389**.

414

You edge around the clearing until you are behind the scaly humanoid and silently glide across the open ground until you are close enough. Placing a needle on your tongue, you spit and it hits it in the back of its neck. The O-Bakemono claps its hand over the wound and roars in pain. It turns to you and scoops up its club. You stare, expecting it to topple, but it remains unaffected and hurls its great club at you. This catches you by surprise and you are not quite quick enough in throwing yourself aside; the club grazes your hip, spinning you around with a sharp bruising pain. Lose 3 Endurance. If you are still alive, you see the huge beast falter slightly, a puzzled expression on its face before it gives a bellowing shout and lumbers towards you, mouth wide, yellowed tusks of teeth bared. Quickly, you spit another needle at the creature. It roars in pain and staggers again. You spit once more and the O-Bakemono falls to its knees and then onto its face in the grass. It has taken enough venom for six men. Turn to **216**.

415

The map which you took from Yaemon, Grandmaster of Flame shows little detail of these lands, so you decide to climb the tallest of the hills to spy out the lie of the land. The top of the hill is unusually flat. Before you reach the crest you hear a shout of horror, but cannot see the man who uttered it. You move forward stealthily and a strange sight greets your eyes. Four young men leap to their feet in surprise as a ghostly faceless figure in blackened, rusted mail, like a long-buried but preserved Barbarian Warlord, seems to drift above the ground towards them from the entrance of an ancient burial mound. One runs towards it, sword drawn. 'No

Vespers, it will take your soul!' roars a priest in white. A third steps forward diffidently and casts a spell which causes a cloud of yellow gas to blossom around the fighter and the apparition, as a fourth man with a green shield and cloak, each bearing a white cross, hurls a war-hammer. The man in white strides forward whirling a flail of spiked chains and the boiling fog of gas swallows all of them up bar the magician who cast the spell.

Will you run to help them (turn to **397**) or wait, unseen, and watch (turn to **351**)?

416

Your reflexes take over and you slap the egg aside with your hand. It curls through the air and shatters against the wall, staining it with pepper and other substances that are already eating into the wall. A device to blind, something unknown by the Ninjas of the Island of Tranquil Dreams.

'Very good,' he says sarcastically. 'One could almost believe that you had some sort of training as a Ninja after all, despite the paltry Way you follow.'

Wasting no time in speech, you take the chance to spring forward and attack. Will you try the Forked Lightning Strike kick (turn to **55**), the Tiger's Paw chop (turn to **304**) or the Whirlpool throw (turn to **87**)?

251

417

You reach the shore and, after a brief rest, run on through the day for many hours, following the shoreline of the Sea of the Star. When you are sure you have lost the men of Quench-heart Keep you decide to spend a day and night recuperating after your ordeal. When you rise early next morning the sun's warmth and the salty air are invigorating. Your rest has done you good. Restore up to 4 points of lost Endurance. After a few days' travel, you come to the river Flatwater and you follow it upstream for some time before heading west, skirting a wooded range of tall mountains. The only beings of any interest that you espy are a few stocky mountain dwarves like small specks on a far away hill-top. After two days' travel you leave the woodlands behind and climb towards a line of conical hills. Turn to 415.

418

The gleaming Sun-Star ring explodes in your face; lose 4 Endurance. The magician must have told you the wrong magical word of command. But, if you are still alive, you see that a Sun-Star has erupted from the ring as you intended and Thaum lies motionless on the damp cellar floor. Your natural cunning, cleverly attacking the magician before he could cast a spell, will stand you in good stead if you live. You may add 1 to the Attack Modifier of your choice. Cassandra cries out in rage while Tyutchev turns to help the fallen magician and she advances quickly to the attack. Turn to 121.

419

You launch yourself feet first and your ankles snap together on either side of the swart goblin's neck but he sits down suddenly and you realise that, though short, he is surprisingly powerful. He braces his broad shoulders and you cannot spin him. Before you have toppled him, the Dancing Sword pierces through your midriff and out through your back. You fall dead, leaving the Goblin King to puzzle as to what magicks are contained in the Scrolls of Kettsuin.

420

At long last the golden shores of the Island of Tranquil Dreams shimmer beyond the breaking waves like a mirage. The ship grinds gently onto the sand and you leap down at the sea's edge and walk towards the great red rock that rests alone in the desert. The temple to Kwon nestles beneath it, its darkest vaults deep within its confines. Before the tiger-head doors stands the Grandmaster of the Dawn. You bow and present the Scrolls of Kettsuin, saying the words of time honoured ritual, 'I have completed my mission, Grandmaster of Grandmasters.' He places his hand on your shoulder and says, 'You are the saviour of all that is good on Orb, even of the temple itself. I named you truly, Avenger. You will be the scourge of injustice for as long as you live.'

There is a great feast in your honour that evening and the villagers cheer you to the echo while Gorobei tells them of your exploits. The children dance around you and you are festooned with flowers

You rest, alone, on the next day until the Grandmaster of the Dawn comes to your cell He squats low on the floor beside you and says, 'Honoric still lives. He has sworn vengeance. He survived even the Blood of Nil, though he was near death for some weeks. Word has just reached us that the Legion of the Sword of Doom prepares once more for war. But enough of this; you cannot bear the cares of the world on your shoulders at all times – come there is little left that I can teach you, but what I can I will. Tomorrow I will tell you something that has been hidden from you. The time has come for me to tell you who your parents were, who you are, you who have become Avenger, the most deadly warrior of them all.'

ALSO AVAILABLE FROM KNIGHT BOOKS